Rec
July 2012

AUG 2012

G... Green

KT-142-686

30131 05038485 5

LONDON BOROUGH OF BARNET

THE FIX

DAMIAN THOMPSON

THE FIX

HOW ADDICTION IS INVADING OUR LIVES AND TAKING OVER YOUR WORLD

Collins

First published in 2012 by Collins
an imprint of HarperCollins*Publishers*
77–85 Fulham Palace Road,
London W6 8JB

www.harpercollins.co.uk

10 9 8 7 6 5 4 3 2 1

Copyright © Damian Thompson 2012

Damian Thompson asserts the moral right to
be identified as the author of this work

A catalogue record of this book is
available from the British Library

ISBN 978-0-00-743608-8 (hardback)
ISBN 978-0-00-743609-5 (paperback)

Printed and bound in Great Britain by
Clays Ltd, St Ives plc

All rights reserved. No part of this publication may be
reproduced, stored in a retrieval system, or transmitted,
in any form or by any means, electronic, mechanical,
photocopying, recording or otherwise, without the prior
written permission of the publishers.

MIX
Paper from
responsible sources
FSC
www.fsc.org
FSC™ C007454

FSC™ is a non-profit international organisation established to promote
the responsible management of the world's forests. Products carrying the
FSC label are independently certified to assure customers that they come
from forests that are managed to meet the social, economic and
ecological needs of present and future generations,
and other controlled sources.

Find out more about HarperCollins and the environment at
www.harpercollins.co.uk/green

CONTENTS

ACKNOWLEDGEMENTS

I'm extremely grateful to my terrific agent, Simon Trewin, for encouraging me to write this book. I was also very lucky to have had Helena Nicholls as my editor at HarperCollins: I've never worked with someone with such a sharp eye for a flabby argument or a non sequitur. My *Telegraph* colleagues Will Heaven and Andrew Brown patiently endured the endless rewrites I asked them to cast their eyes over and saved me from many clumsy errors. In America, my old friend Tim Perkins provided unstinting moral support; Dr Adi Jaffe – whose remarkable story is told in the final chapter – helped me draw the dots between the worlds of drug dealing and academia; and, once again, my dear mentor Prof Stephen O'Leary of the University of Southern California offered generous hospitality while helping me clarify my thoughts.

1

CUPCAKES, IPHONES AND VICODIN

The 21st-century cupcake is a thing of wonder: a modest base of sponge groaning under an indulgently thick layer of frosted sugar or buttercream. It's made to look like a miniature children's birthday cake – and, indeed, birthdays are the perfect excuse to scurry down to the local boutique bakery for a big box of them. The retro charm of cupcakes helps suppress any anxieties you might have about sugar and fat. Your mother made them! Or so the advertising suggests. Perhaps your own mother didn't actually bake cupcakes, but the cutesy pastel-coloured icing implies that one bite will take you back to your child-hood. This can't possibly be junk food, can it?

Now let's consider another ubiquitous presence in modern life: the iPhone, which started out as a self-conscious statement of coolness but which, thanks to Apple's marketing genius, has now become as commonplace as a set of car keys. Millions of people own iPhones, making use of hundreds of thousands of apps, whose functions range from GPS-assisted mapping to compulsively time-wasting computer games. Your iPhone does everything you could require of a mobile phone and more, so you really don't need the upgraded model that Apple has just released … do you?

Then there's Vicodin. It's the most commonly prescribed painkiller in America. In fact, it's the most commonly prescribed *drug* in America: 130 million scripts for it were handed out in 2010 and 244 million for the overall class of drug, narcotic analgesics.[1] It's strong stuff, a mixture of two painkillers: hydrocodone (an addictive opioid) and paracetamol (non-addictive, but causes liver damage in high doses). Vicodin is intended for the sort of pain that makes you cry out in the doctor's waiting room – caused by twisted backs, rotting wisdom teeth and terminal cancer. If they swallow so many of those pills, it seems reasonable to conclude that Americans must be in a lot of pain. Or is it just that millions of people can't manage without Vicodin's deliciously soothing euphoria, even if there's nothing much wrong with them?

A cupcake, a smartphone and a common painkiller. These three objects are so innocent-looking that you could leave them on your desk at work and no one would comment (though the cake might disappear). You can easily consume all three simultaneously: swallow the pill for your bad back with a slurp of coffee while checking your text messages and picking at that yummy frosted topping.

On the other hand, each of these mundane items can get us into trouble. They are objects of desire that can reinforce addictive behaviour – the sort that creeps up on you when your defences are down. That's the subject of this book: a social environment in which more and more of us are being pulled towards some form of addiction, even though we may be unaware of the fact and never become full-blown addicts.

It's not obvious to us now, but the most far-reaching social development of the early 21st century is our increasingly insistent habit of rewarding ourselves whenever we feel the need to lift our moods.

When our hand creeps out towards yet another square of organic chocolate, or when we play just one more game of Angry Birds before setting off for work, or when we check a secretly bookmarked porn site for new arrivals, we're behaving like addicts. The activity in question can be innocent or shameful. Either way, it reinforces the addictive streak in human nature.

That streak is there because our brains have evolved to seek out immediate, short-term rewards. Our ancestors needed to stuff themselves with energy-rich berries and to respond quickly to sexual stimulation; we wouldn't be here if they hadn't.

Our problem is that we've built an environment that bombards us with rewards that our bodies don't need and that do nothing to ensure our survival as a species. Yet, because they are rewards – that is, because they provoke specific feelings of anticipation and pleasure in the brain – we grab them anyway.

To put it another way, we reach out for a fix.

That's a word we associate with helpless addicts. They talk about their 'fix' because it feels as if they've temporarily fixed themselves when they take their drug of choice. There's no mystery about this. As a result of heavy exposure to the drug, they have become dependent on frequent chemical rewards. Their brains are in a state of hyper-vigilance, waiting for the blessed relief of a chemical that, once tolerance develops, merely allows the addict to feel normal, as opposed to anxious and ill.

That much is not in dispute. Many addiction specialists go further, however. They say that the brains of addicts are fundamentally different from those of non-addicts. They are *forced* to chase these rewards because they have 'the disease of addiction'.

This book challenges that theory. It suggests that, if you keep eating chocolate biscuits until you feel sick, you're indulging in a milder version of the addictive behaviour that leads heroin addicts to overdose. I'm not equating the two situations, of course. I'm suggesting that they lie at different points on a spectrum of addictive behaviour on which everyone can be located.

Also, and more importantly, many of us are being pulled towards the dangerous end of the spectrum, thanks to technological and social changes that stimulate the most fundamental of all our instincts – desire.

Never before have we had access to so many desirable things and experiences that we hope will change our moods. I know 'things and experiences' sounds vague, but that's really the point. Addiction has never been confined to substance abuse, and with each passing week technology unveils a new object, process or relationship we can obsess over.

CUPCAKES, IPHONES AND VICODIN

For example, these days our fixes are often delivered to us through social networking tools such as Facebook or Twitter that enable us to manipulate our circle of friends. Installing and deleting people as if they were iPhone apps offers a quick and dirty method of changing our feelings (though, needless to say, we are furious when someone deletes us). It's a consumer experience.

In any discussion of addiction, whether of the trivial or life-threatening variety, the concept of desire is just as important as that of pleasure. Usually, it's more important. That's because the anticipation of the fix is more powerful than the moment of consumption, which often fails to live up to expectations. Sometimes we throw internal tantrums when this happens. The fix infantilises us so that, like children, we are constantly and annoyingly hungry for more.

Believe me, I speak from experience.

●

I spent many years as an addict. I was pathetically addicted to alcohol between the ages of 18 and 32. It took me a long time to acknowledge the fact, though – to realise that the act of getting drunk delighted and obsessed me to a degree that set me apart from most of my friends and colleagues. My doctor tells me I'm still an addict. I'm not exactly happy to wear that label after spending such a long time avoiding so much as a sip of alcohol, but the evidence is compelling. Since giving up drinking, my addictive desires have attached themselves to one thing, person or experience after another. I can't swallow a Nurofen Plus for a headache without hoping that I'll enjoy a little codeine buzz. I can obsess for ten minutes in front of a display of confectionery in a newsagent's. And my CD-buying habit has nearly bankrupted me. Trivial stuff compared with my drinking, but my over-reactions to these stimulations don't feel normal, exactly.

Perhaps *the* crucial feature of addiction is the progressive replacement of people by things. That deceptively simple statement is a brilliant insight, though I can't claim credit for it. It comes from Craig Nakken, author of a bestselling book called *The Addictive Personality*, who argues that addicts form primary relationships with objects and events, not with people.

He writes: 'Normally, we manipulate objects for our own pleasure, to make life easier. Addicts slowly transfer this style of relating to objects to their interactions with people, treating them as one-dimensional objects to manipulate as well.'

What begins as an attempt to find emotional fulfilment ends up turning in on itself. Why? Because the addict comes to judge other people simply in terms of how useful they are in delivering a fix. And, at some stage, everybody lets you down. Therefore the addict concludes that objects are more dependable than people. Objects have no wants or needs. 'In a relationship with an object the addict can always come first,' says Nakken.[2]

I felt a shiver of recognition when I first read those words. But it wasn't just my own behaviour that came to mind, or that of people whom society can conveniently label 'addicts'. This may come across as a presumptuous thing to say, but over the last decade I've been struck by the way friends and colleagues, most of them psychologically far healthier than me, have begun to display aspects of the process Nakken describes. Lifestyle accessories exert an ever greater power over them, disrupting relationships, nurturing obsessions and – as I've noticed in the office – dominating conversation.

Does that mean that the people around me are turning into addicts? That's never an easy question to answer, because 'addict' is such a loaded term. It's a good word to describe people whose problems are obviously out of control, as mine were, but it has to be used carefully. Not only does it carry misleading overtones of disease, but it also implies that there's a clear dividing line between 'addicts' and 'non-addicts'. That's not true. In my experience, addiction is something that people *do* – to themselves and other people – rather than something that just happens to them; it's not like developing cancer.

Addiction is easier to understand as a concept if we focus on clearly observable behaviour – that is, the search for a fix and its consequences. Almost anyone can indulge in addictive behaviour, but some of us are more prone to it than others, for reasons that scientists don't fully understand.

In fact, let's get this point out of the way right at the beginning of this book. In the past couple of decades, countless scientific studies have attempted to pinpoint what it is about either the brains or the upbringings of addicts that leads them to adopt self-destructive lifestyles. They have failed to do so.

No one is immune from developing addictive behaviour. If there's a history of addiction in your family, you're more at risk. Likewise, if you have an impulsive personality – that is, score highly for 'impulsivity' in psychological tests – you're more likely to do something impulsive, such as try a new drug or drink that fatal last glass of whisky before jumping into your car. Indeed, a fashionable term for various addictions is 'impulse control disorders'.[3]

For me these findings fall into the 'No shit, Sherlock' category of scientific discoveries. They tell us nothing very surprising. The consensus at the moment is that addiction seems to be the product of genetic inheritance and environment. In other words, the nature versus nurture question is no closer to being settled in this area of human biology than it is in any other. To repeat: we're all at risk. That's why the contents of this book apply to everyone, not just coke-snorting hedge fund managers, bulimic receptionists and absent fathers glued to World of Warcraft.

Psychologists talk about addictive behaviours in the plural, recognising the many different impulses that tempt people. What these behaviours tend to have in common is the replacement of people by things and events. We all develop these habits to a certain degree; the people we call addicts are those people who can't or won't give them up even when they cause harm to themselves and others. Again, that's a loose definition, fuzzy at the edges. Never mind; addiction isn't an easy phenomenon to pin down.

This isn't to deny that addictive behaviour has important consequences for the brain. It does. Indeed, it can partly be explained by the overstimulation of the brain's fearsomely complex reward circuitry.

Different parts of the human brain govern what some scientists call the Stop and Go impulses. More primitive sections of the brain – parts that we share with other animals – tell us to consume as much as possible in order to increase our chances of survival. They say: Go. More highly developed parts of the brain, capable of reasoning and not found in other animals, hold up a Stop sign when we're consuming too much of something for our own good. Classic addicts keep ignoring the Stop instruction, despite the high cost to themselves and others. They require instant gratification, whatever the consequences. Indeed, they'll often seize any opportunity to indulge in addictive behaviour even when there's no real gratification to be extracted from it. We'll discuss this puzzling paradox later.

The Stop and Go imagery helps us understand the growing appeal of the fix. As technologies develop and converge, the speed of delivery increases. So does the speed of our expectations. We now live in a world filled with life-enhancing objects and substances that promise ever faster and more effective gratification. It's as if everything that tumbles off a production line is stamped with the word Go.

Temptation peeks out at us from the strangest places. Who would have guessed, 40 years ago, that a piece of electronic office equipment – the personal computer – would morph into something so desirable that people would sacrifice huge chunks of their spare time (and income) in order to play with it? Or that modifications to a telephone would generate global excitement?

Changes to our appetites don't come about by accident. The manager of your local Starbucks didn't wake up one morning and think: 'I know what would brighten up my customers' afternoons – an ice-blended cappuccino!' As we'll see, the Frappuccino was invented when Starbucks employed food technology to solve a specific business challenge. As a result, hundreds of thousands of their customers (including me) developed a near-obsessive relationship with something they had previously lived happily without.

The pace of technological change means we need to revise our concept of addiction. Our cultural history provides us with images of stereotypical addicts, some of them dating back centuries: the grinning harridan dropping her baby down a staircase in Hogarth's *Gin Lane*; the American Indians crazed with 'firewater'; the hollow-eyed Chinese sailor propped against the wall of an opium den; the junkie shivering in an alleyway surrounded by needles. Also, anyone who lives in a city is used to the sight of spectacular drunks and morbidly obese people whose addictions are so grotesquely out of control that we avert our eyes.

These are powerful images, but if we pay too much attention to them then we can end up with a dangerous sense of immunity. We overlook our own eagerness to self-administer fixes, those sensory experiences that temporarily lift the mood while subtly detaching us from traditional human relationships. The fix can take any number of forms. Some toy very obviously with the chemistry of the brain.

CUPCAKES, IPHONES AND VICODIN

Anyone with a rolled banknote up their nose knows that – so long as their dealer hasn't ripped them off – they're about to experience the effects of a mind-altering substance. The same goes for the guy swigging from a whisky bottle. In contrast, the tubby young man who demolishes a packet of chocolate digestives while watching the football doesn't suspect that his eating habits have left his brain unusually sensitive to stimulation by sugar; he just knows that, once the packet's opened, the biscuits disappear. His habit of stuffing his face with refined sugar and vegetable fat doesn't place him very far along the addictive spectrum – but, then again, it may be enough to put him in intensive care when he has a heart attack at 50.

The most puzzling addictions are those that don't involve the consumption of any substance. Gambling is the obvious example – we've known for hundreds of years that it can tear apart families as ruthlessly as hard liquor. In academic circles, these non-substance addictions are known as 'process addictions'. It's now clear that things you don't eat, drink, smoke or inject can nevertheless disturb your brain in much the same way as drugs. And, in an age when so much digital entertainment – notably video games and online pornography – is designed to be as addictive as possible, their potential to do this is accelerating rapidly.

The global marketplace offers a bewildering selection of consumer experiences, simultaneously delightful and dangerous. It's constantly modifying products and experiences that were never previously considered to be addictive – or simply didn't exist until recently.

Also, as we'll see, corporations have learned how to supercharge old-established intoxicants by popularising new patterns of consuming them. One vivid example is the phenomenon of recreational binge drinking, particularly by women. People have always got drunk, and a minority have always enjoyed going on binges with their friends. What no one predicted was the emergence of the binge as everyday behaviour. Ordinary drinkers, with no history of a problem with alcohol, now plan evenings to end in a messy and helpless surrender to the drug. And this is seen as *normal*.

It would be silly to pretend that everyone is equally threatened by this changing style of consumption. But the prospect of whole populations learning new ways of tampering with the flow of pleasure-giving chemicals in their brains is one that should make us feel very uneasy.

With that in mind, let's take another look at the cake, the phone and the pill.

●

In 1996 a tiny corner shop called the Magnolia Bakery opened in Manhattan's West Village. Its old-fashioned cakes and pies quickly became the objects of guilty fantasy for women who liked to pretend that nothing more fattening than tuna carpaccio ever passed their lips. Then, in 2000, the bakery featured in an episode of *Sex and the City*. This was the moment America's cupcake craze began in earnest.

In the episode, Carrie and Miranda were filmed sitting outside the Magnolia. Carrie, played by Sarah Jessica Parker, told her friend that there was a new obsession in her life. This turned out to be a new boyfriend called Aidan – but viewers could have been forgiven for thinking it was icing sugar, judging by the way Parker was pushing the rose-coloured cupcake into her face. Viewed in slow motion, it's a faintly disgusting spectacle. The truth is, there's no elegant way to eat a Magnolia cupcake, which is why customers adopt self-mocking smiles as the fluorescent globules of frosting tumble down their chins.

'When Carrie took her first bite, she left teeth marks in my neighbourhood,' wrote Emma Forrest, a journalist living opposite the bakery. 'Not long after the episode was broadcast, the tourists started to arrive and the bakery started charging them if they wanted to take photographs of Carrie and co's favourite haunt. With the influx of tourists came the rats, as half-eaten cupcakes were dumped into overflowing bins outside my apartment … Riding on this extraordinary upturn in its fortunes, Magnolia changed its hours, and stayed open to midnight throughout the summer. I was kept awake each night by the hoots and hollers coming from the queue that now snakes all the way around the block.'[4]

In 2006 and 2007 I spent quite a lot of time in the West Village visiting my friend Harry Mount, then New York correspondent of the *Daily Telegraph*. By this time, *Sex and the City* was off the air and the cupcake craze had gone mainstream: Magnolia-style bakeries were opening all over America. Yet, on chilly autumn evenings, there was still a queue outside the original store, and it didn't seem to consist of tourists. 'Our local stick-thin fashion victims can't get enough of the things,' explained Harry. In which case, how come they were stick-thin? Was there a parking lot at the back where they threw them up?

That was a bad-taste private joke between Harry and me, but when I recently did a word search on 'cupcakes' and 'bulimia' I discovered a blog by a bulimic mother of two entitled 'Eating Cupcakes in the Parking Lot'. Its posts appear to have been deleted, but cupcakes feature prominently in many other blogs devoted to eating disorders. After a row with her boyfriend, one bulimic girl baked cupcakes decorated with the words 'I am sorry'. She added mournfully: 'And now where are those cupcakes? Floating along a sewage pipe.'5

This sort of incident isn't unusual. Abigail Natenshon, a psychotherapist who treats eating disorders, tells another horror story involving cupcakes: 'One young woman with bulimia found herself, at a time of great stress, compelled to drive into a 7–11 convenience store where she purchased three cupcakes; she then proceeded to stuff them down her throat whole in an emotional frenzy in the dark and deserted alley behind the store. As far as she was concerned, her binge had begun at the moment when she drove her car up to the front door and did not finish until she had purged the cupcakes.'6

The disturbing subculture of 'pro-ana' (pro-anorexia) websites actually encourages girls to starve themselves, or 'b/p' (binge and purge). A recurring question on these sites is: are cupcakes easy to throw up? Answer: not as easy as ice cream, but eating them with diet soda can help.

'It doesn't surprise me that cupcakes are favourites with bulimics,' the food writer Xanthe Clay told me. 'They're the ultimate eye-candy, primped and styled like a teen pop star, the food incarnation of many girls' fantasies.

'In the gossip magazine world, where shopping is the only serious rival to celebrity in terms of aspiration, cupcakes are consumer-desirable in a way a Victoria sponge isn't. If having an eating disorder is about a desperate attempt to take control, then eating these artificial, too-perfect creations may be particularly satisfying. More likely, the huge sugar rush will feed the craving, and provide a quivering kick of hypoglycaemia. The texture – smooth, aerated, oily – may, like ice cream, be especially suitable for regurgitation.

'And – just my prejudice this – but perhaps the ultimate emptiness of cupcakes, those empty calories, the way they never deliver on flavour what they promise in looks, is a metaphor for the hopelessness of the woman, or man, with bulimia.'

Although a high proportion of bulimics have 'issues' with cupcakes, clearly the overwhelming majority of people who eat them don't throw them up. They do, however, seem obsessed with them. A chain called Crumbs sells 1.5 million cupcakes *every month* in 35 US stores; in June 2011, it started trading on the Nasdaq, with an opening valuation of $59 million. And market analysts predict robust growth if Crumbs moves into emerging markets such as China.

The Facebook group for Sprinkles Cupcakes had, at the time of writing, been 'liked' by 325,000 people and was spreading the cupcake gospel with near-hysterical enthusiasm.[7] For Valentine's Day: 'It's back! The first 50 people to whisper "love at first bite" at each Sprinkles receive a free raspberry chocolate chip!' For Super Sunday: 'Whether you're rooting for the New York Giants or New England Patriots or just tuning in for the commercials, Sprinkles Super Sunday boxes will score a touchdown at any viewing party. Each box contains 6 Red Velvet and 6 Vanilla cupcakes, adorned with football sugar decorations and your favourite team's name. Just don't get tackled reaching for the last one!' There were even signs that cupcakes were trying to infiltrate the military-industrial complex: 'Sprinkles is excited to bring freshly baked cupcakes to the Pentagon! Pentagon employees can find us in the Main Concourse ...'

This is a resilient craze, as Dana Cowin, *Food & Wine* magazine's editor-in-chief told Reuters in 2011. 'I have predicted the demise of the cupcake so many times that I'm actually going to go to the dark side now and say the cupcake trend is not going to abate,' she said.[8] When an earthquake struck Washington DC on 23 August 2011, someone tweeted that you could tell it had happened because there was suddenly no line outside Georgetown Cupcakes.

Could the 'emptiness' of the cupcakes to which Xanthe Clay refers be part of their appeal? Their overwhelming sugar hit fills the consumer with what nutritionists call 'empty calories', because they have no nutritional value. But that's not to say they have no mood-altering value. Sugar triggers production of the brain's natural opioids, according to Princeton neuroscientist Bart Hobel, who led a study into sugar dependence. He found that rats which binged on sugar went into withdrawal when the supply was cut off. 'We think that is a key to the addiction process,' he said. 'The brain is getting addicted to its own opioids as it would to morphine or heroin. Drugs give a bigger effect, but it is essentially the same process.'[9]

Opioids are also implicated in bulimia, irrespective of whether sugar is involved. Have you ever experienced that feeling of glorious relief after you've just thrown up a dodgy curry? It's not just getting rid of the food that makes you feel good; it's a natural elation produced by chemicals in the brain. Bulimics get off on it, to put it crudely.

As Abigail Natenshon explains: 'The bulimic cycle releases endorphins, [opioid] brain chemicals that infuse a person with a sense of numbness or euphoria. Ironically, the relief passes in short order, only to be replaced by anxiety and guilt for the bulimic behaviours.' Again, we need to state the obvious fact that most people don't throw up their food. But the sort of food associated with purging is also the sort of food that many of us have difficulty resisting, because its heavy concentrations of sugar, fat or salt can magnify euphoria and neediness.

It's easy for urban sophisticates to mock American rednecks or British 'chavs' who stuff themselves with fast food, and easy to recognise that they're in the grip of some sort of addiction. Just look at their waistlines. But the marketing executive who orders a cranberry muffin to go with her morning cup of coffee really ought to ask herself: why am I eating cake for breakfast?

●

So what about the iPhone? Isn't it a bit much to call our love affair with this shiny gadget an 'addiction'? Researchers at Stanford University aren't so sure: in a survey of 200 Stanford students in 2010, 44 per cent of respondents said they were either very or completely addicted to their smartphones.[10] Nine per cent admitted to 'patting' their iPhone. Eight per cent recalled thinking that their iPods were 'jealous' of their iPhones. These are strange things for students at one of America's top universities to say about their phones, even in jest. They also reveal something about how completely the iPhone has become part of these students' identities and social frameworks. They're not just tools that allow us to connect instantaneously and prolifically with others: they're also being afforded identities of their own – 'patted', protected and cherished.

Perhaps it has something to do with how these devices are engineered. They practically *force* you to perform repetitive rituals of the sort associated with obsessive-compulsive behaviour: from the initial activation of the iPhone to the weekly 'syncing' and nightly charging, your relationship to the phone is structured for you. And because the iPhone's battery life isn't quite enough to last a full day's use – and certainly not long enough to withstand hours of constant fiddling and gaming – 'pit stop' charges become a regular feature of the day. iPhone users can often be seen checking for power sockets in coffee shops so that, while they get their own fix of caffeine, their phones can get juiced up as well.

'iPhone owners live in a constant state of anxiety about their battery levels,' says Milo Yiannopoulos, editor of *The Kernel*, an online culture magazine. 'To some extent, the phone ends up structuring their day. For example, they tend not to plan to be out of the office for more than six hours at a time, in case they run out of battery and have to start knocking on doors, USB cable in hand, begging for a few minutes' worth of charge to get them through the afternoon.'

Talk about the replacement of people by things. The 4S version of the iPhone, released in October 2011, includes a virtual assistant called Siri that responds to spoken instructions and speaks back to the user. This infant technology is already so complex that you can have entire conversations with Siri. She will then execute commands, in some cases fetching very specific data from the internet. 'Intelligent person-alised assistant software is going mainstream,' says Yiannopoulos. 'Never in the history of mass-market consumer electronics has the line between man and machine been so blurred.'

It's significant that a quarter of respondents in the survey above said they found iPhones 'dangerously alluring'. They are supposed to be. Absolutely nothing is left to chance in the design of these devices. If Apple customers have an embarrassing tendency to anthropomorphise their gadgets, that is because Apple has explored the possibilities of the human mind and body more thoroughly than any of its competitors.

For example, one of the most appealing features of the MacBook laptop line has been the status light, which pulsates gently when the computer is sleeping. Early reviewers cooed over the calming effect of the light, but couldn't put their finger on why it felt so good to watch. Later, it was revealed that Apple had filed for a patent for a sleep-mode indicator that 'mimics the rhythm of breathing' and was therefore 'psychologically appealing'. As the tech blogger Jesse Young noted, while Apple's sleep light matched the pace of breathing while we sleep, Dell's was closer to breathing during strenuous exercise. 'It's interesting how a lot of companies try to copy Apple but never seem to get it right. This is yet another example of Apple's obsessive attention to detail,' he wrote.[11]

Former Apple executives – who frequently brief American technology blogs off the record about the internal culture at Apple's headquarters in Cupertino, California – describe the lengths the organisation goes to in order to create coveted products. There's a design-dominated power structure that results in hushed reverence when Jonathan Ive, Senior Vice President of Industrial Design, walks into the boardroom. 'Marketing and design have been fused into a single discipline at Apple,' says Yiannopoulos. 'Everything, from product strategy to research and development, is subordinate to making the products as beautiful and compulsive – that is, as addictive – as possible.'

It works. To quote an extreme example, in 2010 a schoolboy in Taiwan was diagnosed with IAD – iPhone Addiction Disorder. According to Dr Tsung-tsai Yang of the Cardinal Tien Hospital, his eyes were glued to his phone screen all day and all night. Eventually, 'the boy had to be hospitalised in a mental ward after his daily life was thrown into complete disarray by his iPhone addiction'.[12]

Two days after it opened in 2010, I visited the Apple Store in Covent Garden – a magnificently restored Palladian building dominated by a glass-covered courtyard. The heady aroma of addiction was unmistakable. The misery in the queue for the Genius Bar, where broken computers are diagnosed, was painful to behold. Legs were crossed and uncrossed and eyebrows twitched every time a Genius read out a name. I couldn't help thinking that these customers looked like addicts waiting for their daily dose of methadone.

I wanted to ask a Genius what it was like dealing with people who weren't just asking what was wrong with their laptops but pleading for (literal) fixes. But finding someone who would talk was easier said than done.

First I went down the route of asking an Apple Store manager – a friend of a friend – whether he could chat off the record about the way the company seemed to encourage addiction to its products, or put me in touch with someone who would. His first response was encouraging, but then he changed his mind. He would be in big trouble if his bosses suspected he'd put me in touch with an indiscreet ex-employee, and he'd be fired on the spot if he got caught blabbing himself.

So I tried a different route. A start-up CEO friend of mine put out a message to one of his networks. Shortly afterwards, a young man called Ben Jackson, a social media entrepreneur, emailed to say he could meet me for coffee in Soho, London, a few streets from the Apple Store where he had spent two years as a Genius.

Ben, like many former Apple employees, inhabited the cooler end of the geek spectrum, with glasses offset by a gym-honed body. He didn't need any prompting to talk about addiction to technology: the experience of seeing the addiction every day – deliberately stimulated by the company – was one of the reasons he left the store.

'I saw a whole range of addictive behaviours. It's one of the things that made the Apple Store such a surreal place to work. At one end of the scale you have the total Apple obsessives who exhibit a sort of religious fanaticism that the company does nothing to discourage – it encourages it, in fact. They're the people who will book the same tutorial again and again, being shown how to do stuff they already know.

'When a new product is launched, it's the same faces at the front of the line every time. They treat the staff almost like celebrities, trying to ingratiate themselves. At the Genius Bar, they'll show you Apple products from years ago, and you'll have to pretend you haven't seen them before, because they need their egos massaged. It's kind of sad. Well, it *is* sad.'

But it's not only the true obsessives who are touched by addiction, according to Ben. 'There's a general perception that Apple is awesome in a way that other companies aren't – a perception that's quite at odds with the way it operates behind the scenes. Even the products are considered awesome, which is why otherwise normal people would get quite disproportionately angry and upset if anything went wrong with them. And it's also why there's such unease if people think they've fallen behind, that their stuff is out of date. But the point is that you can't keep up to date without spending a lot of money on things you don't need, because the products are just coming out too fast.

CUPCAKES, IPHONES AND VICODIN

'I've seen people burst into tears because a credit check wouldn't allow them to stretch to the latest upgrade. That's when I started thinking: I need to get the hell out of here.'

Admittedly, many psychiatrists don't believe in 'internet addiction' as a medical condition, let alone addiction to a specific model of smartphone. They argue that obsessive users aren't addicted to the internet so much as to the experiences it provides, such as digital porn and computer games. But few experts would deny that gadgets such as iPhones can produce behaviour that bears the hallmarks of addiction. And it's becoming increasingly clear that the ability of manufacturers to stimulate this behaviour is racing far ahead of our ability to cope with the psychological and social problems that are created as a result.

The science of pleasure is playing a greater role in the marketing strategies of all sorts of companies: the people who waft the smell of freshly baked doughnuts at you in the shopping mall have fine-tuned their recipes in the laboratory, not the kitchen. But Apple is in a class of its own. No other company has managed to mix such a finely balanced cocktail of desire, in which the crude flavour of compulsion is disguised by a deliciously minimalist aesthetic.

'More than any other product, the iPhone has encouraged the tech industry to concentrate on getting people hooked on things,' says Yiannopoulos. 'Apple's marketing genius, and the incredible attention to detail paid to the design of their devices, filters down into the iPhone developer ecosystem.'

He cites the example of Angry Birds, a simple computer game app that, by May 2011, had been downloaded 200 million times.[13] The premise of Angry Birds is simple: players launch birds across the screen with a slingshot, judging the trajectory of flight and altering the force and initial direction accordingly. It sounds harmless enough. But type 'Angry Birds addiction' into Google and you're presented with 3.24 million results. So many people complain about being addicted to the game that it has spawned self-help pages all over the internet. Some of these pages ask whether Angry Birds addictions are changing people's brains. Self-described addicts say they don't know why they can't put the game down, and talk about compulsively tracing their fingers on tables as they subconsciously recall the catapult action of the game. These sound suspiciously like the little rituals associated with alcoholism and drug abuse.

Again, perhaps a degree of scepticism is called for: it can only be a matter of time before some opportunistic researcher diagnoses ABAD – Angry Birds Addiction Disorder (which would presumably be a particular strain of IAD, since the game is played mostly on iPhones). No doubt the Angry Birds craze will fade, as these crazes always do. But it may well leave behind a residue, in the form of the compulsive instinct to perform repetitive actions.

It's not a conspiracy theory to suggest that the primary task of iPhone game developers is learning how to manipulate our brains' reward circuits. They cheerfully admit as much. At the 2010 Virtual Goods Summit in London, Peter Vesterbacka, lead developer for

Rovio, the company behind Angry Birds, described how they make the game so addictive. 'We use simple A/B testing to work out what keeps people coming back,' he said. 'We don't have to guess any more. With so many users, we can just run the numbers.'[14]

We can just run the numbers. Remember those words. Where previously advertising and marketing were more creative disciplines that involved a huge element of risk, a new generation of manufacturers doesn't need to guess what will keep us coming back for our fix: they already know.

●

Viewers of *House*, America's most popular medical drama – and at one time the most watched television programme in the world – are familiar with the sight of Dr Gregory House, the snide, sexy, crippled anti-hero, tipping back his head and tossing a couple of Vicodin into his mouth. He's even been known to throw a pill into the air and catch it like a performing seal. The screenplays go out of their way to portray House as an addict: several times we're shown him shivering and sweating his way through opiate withdrawal. But, in the end, the Vicodin is as integral to his charm as his twisted humour. The one fuels the other.

Although Dr House, played brilliantly by Hugh Laurie, is prescribed the drug to dull the pain of a leg injury, he also uses it to stave off boredom and stimulate his work as a diagnostic detective. Any similarity to the cocaine-injecting Sherlock Holmes is surely intentional. But only the very earliest Holmes stories actually depict drug abuse: Arthur Conan Doyle, worried that he might encourage addiction, quickly made his hero abandon the vice. Not so the makers of *House*, who have sustained the central character's dependence on Vicodin despite criticism from some medical professionals (and, reportedly, the Drug Enforcement Agency).

'Since the first episode I have been concerned with the show's message and have attempted several times to educate the writers and producers regarding the danger of Vicodin abuse,' wrote one physician, coincidentally named Dr John House, who specialises in hearing loss, a devastating side effect of Vicodin.[15] He lobbied long and hard for this symptom to be recognised in *House* and eventually it was, albeit in a throwaway line. (As I write, the series is coming to an end, and so far one symptom that hasn't been mentioned, so far as I can tell, is the awful constipation it causes: a truly realistic scenario would force the good doctor to spend most of the season straining on the lavatory.) The fictional House does succeed in giving up Vicodin after suffering rather implausible hallucinations caused by the drug and completing a period of rehab, but after a couple of seasons he is shown relapsing.

Vicodin was already a fashionable recreational drug when the show first aired in 2004. It was passed around like after-dinner mints at Manhattan dinner parties. In 2001, *USA Today* described Vicodin as 'the new celebrity drug of choice'. Matthew Perry, one of the stars of *Friends*, had already gone into rehab for his addiction to it – twice. Eminem had a Vicodin tattoo on his arm. David Spade joked about it at the Golden Globes. 'Who isn't doing them?' asked Courtney Love.

'Everyone who makes it starts popping them.'[16] Celebrities favoured it for the same reason other users did: it was (and is) relatively easy to persuade doctors to prescribe it. In the US, Vicodin falls into the Schedule III category, less tightly controlled than stronger opiate painkillers such as Oxycontin, classified as Schedule II. You can phone in a prescription for Vicodin to a pharmacy; for Oxycontin, you have to hand over a physical script.

So by the time the first *House* screenplays were being written in 2003, Vicodin was already as famous for its recreational buzz as for its painkilling properties. When the show became a hit, Associated Press writer Frazier Moore suggested that its success was thanks to the way it 'fetishises pain'. In other words, millions of Americans on painkillers could identify with Dr House's suffering.[17] If true, that's only part of the story. The scripts often refer to Greg House's pain, caused by the removal of leg muscles after a thigh aneurysm. But much of the sharpest humour centres around House's schoolboy naughtiness in trying to score more pills than he has been prescribed. That isn't the fetishisation of pain: it's the fetishisation of Vicodin. An unofficial range of *House* T-shirts, still on sale in 2011, includes one that reads: 'Wake up and smell the Vicodin'. The same logo, accompanied by a photo of Hugh Laurie looking spaced out, is also available as desktop wallpaper for your computer.

Meanwhile, the embedding of the drug in other parts of popular culture continues apace.

'The Vicodin Song', by singer-songwriter Terra Naomi, has been watched on YouTube more than half a million times. It's an appropriately sleepy ballad which begins: *And I've got Vicodin, do you wanna come over?*

The most popular comment on the thread underneath the YouTube video reads: 'When I listen to this I think of Dr House :)) This song is really cool.'[18] Many of the 2,000-plus comments, however, aren't about the song or the show. They're about how much Vicodin you can take recreationally without hurting your liver. It's a vigorous debate:

FreeWhoopin1390: Well vicodin (aka hydrocodone) gives you a good calm high. It's a super chill high to be honest. Now some people might try and tell you that 20–25 mg gets you high, let me start by saying those people are idiots. 20–25 mg will give you a relaxed small buzz for the first time. If you want a really good calm high that lasts for a while take 35–40 mg. I say 40 for the first time but that's just me. Word of caution tho, do not exceed 4000 mg of tylenol [paracetamol] which is in vicodin, in 24 hours.

Thebluefus: If you get 40 mg of hydrocodone by taking vicodin you have reached the max for tylenol. You don't need that much to get high, especially as a first time. Just two vicodin will get you the feeling. Don't be stupid.

FreeWhoopin1390: Are you fucking stupid? The max for tylenol is 4000 mg a day. I take 50 mg of hydrocodone at once (they are 10/500). Which means they have 10 mg hydrocodone and

500 mg tylenol. Which means I am taking 2500 mg of tylenol. Which is nowhere near the max daily dosage. But thank you for sharing what you don't know.

There are also catfights about the respective virtues of Vicodin and Oxycontin and a discussion of the regional variations in street prices. From time to time someone interrupts to say that they take Vicodin for real pain and that these junkies should be ashamed of themselves. But there are also commenters who were legitimately prescribed the drug who are now junkies themselves. They may resent being a slave to Vicodin or they may enjoy the high; perhaps a bit of both. What should we make of a comment like this?

> *1awareness*: Bragging about pills is lame. I'm using them to make fibromyalgia feel less intense. I also have seizures which cause a lot of pain. I enjoy Vicodin.

These are commenters who describe themselves as Vicodin 'users/abusers', a term that neatly captures the ambiguity of prescription drug abuse. All mood-altering drugs, from Scotch whisky to crack cocaine, can be abused: you can harm yourself by taking too much of them. But the vast majority are *supposed* to intoxicate, even when consumed in 'safe' quantities. The Vicodin abuser, on the other hand, is hooked on a drug that the manufacturers insist isn't designed to alter moods. To further complicate matters, if the abuser is in real pain, it can be hard to tell whether he or she is merely over-medicating or enjoying an extra recreational buzz on top of the pain relief – Dr Gregory House likes to keep his colleagues guessing on this point. But that sort of confusion doesn't make Vicodin dependence any less difficult to manage; it just means that, like so many 21st-century addictions, it is difficult to categorise and therefore difficult to treat.

As if these problems weren't bad enough, it was revealed at the beginning of 2012 that several drug companies were working on hydrocodone pills that were potentially ten times as strong as Vicodin. The new pills would be 'safer' than Vicodin, according to Roger Hawley, chief executive of Zogenix, because they wouldn't contain the paracetamol that harms the liver. Maybe so; but their time-release formula would also allow abusers to crunch them up for one hell of a hit. Zohydro, as Zogenix plans to call the drug, is scheduled for release in 2013.

This is just a guess, but it wouldn't surprise me if, all over America, clued-up Vicodin users are already telling their doctors that their pain is getting worse and maybe they could use something a little stronger …

●

The addictive qualities of cupcakes, iPhones and Vicodin aren't immediately obvious. Someone encountering a cupcake for the first time since childhood doesn't think: uh-oh, I'd better be careful not to develop a sugar addition that triggers an eating disorder and end up washing the sick out of my hair. Likewise, people buying their first smartphone don't worry about developing an obsessive-compulsive relationship with a computer game, and until recently the recreational use of painkillers was almost unheard of. In other words, as unqualified consumers we're increasingly tempted by products about whose effect on our brain we know virtually nothing. We may not even notice the burst of tension-relieving pleasure they provide – at least, not until we realise that we can't live without them.

Using substances and manipulating situations to fix your mood isn't new. It's the pace, intensity, range and scale of this mood-fixing that is unprecedented, irrespective of whether it involves drugs, alcohol, food or sex.

Put simply, both our *need* and our *ability* to manipulate our feelings are growing. We're always searching for new ways to change the way we feel because, to state the obvious, we're not at ease with ourselves. That's a very broad-brush statement, so let me try to be more specific. Our ancestors were unable to insulate themselves from fear and despair in the way that we try to: certain forms of unhappiness, such as grief at the death of children, were more familiar to them than they are to us. Nor did they possess many fixes to address those feelings – and, in any case, experiences of such intensity aren't easily fixed, even in the short term. We, on the other hand, struggle with small but inexorable and cumulative pressures in our daily lives. These produce a free-floating anxiety that *is* susceptible to short-term fixes.

The hi-tech world that ratchets up the pressure on us also yields scientific discoveries that speed up the flow of pleasure-giving and performance-enhancing chemicals in our brains. Indeed, producers and consumers collude vigorously in this process, which helps us cope with commitments that we feel are beyond our control. (Note, incidentally, how the verb 'to cope' has invaded so many areas of human activity: sometimes it seems that we need a 'coping strategy' just to go to the bathroom.) The jokey phrase 'retail therapy' has entered the language for a good reason. We, as consumers, know that the instant gratification of a purchase goes beyond simple pleasure at acquiring something new – it can change the way we feel about everything, albeit only for a short time. Manufacturers are well aware of it, too. They know they are the purveyors of fixes, and that the moment their fixes fail is the moment they start losing market share.

The problem is that these increasingly complex interactions between producers and consumers are also increasingly unpredictable, especially in their effects on the human body. It's not possible to predict with any accuracy the sorts of relationships that people will form with the substances and experiences thrust at them. Neuroscientists are learning new things about our reward systems all the time, but they'll admit privately that the attempt to turn these discoveries into drugs that target specific mental disorders have been shockingly hit-and-miss. Meanwhile, the rest of us know only one thing about those reward systems: how to stimulate them.

In other words, we are sitting in front of the controls of a machine whose workings are basically a mystery to us. And someone has just handed us the ignition keys.

2

IS ADDICTION REALLY A 'DISEASE'?

'When people ask why I don't drink, I explain that I'm allergic to alcohol. But really, it's a disease. We all have it – everyone in this room.'

The speaker was Pippa, a former actress in her sixties with dyed auburn hair and scarlet lipstick applied so thickly that her mouth looked like a clown's. This may sound rude, but of all the AA regulars gathered round the trestle table in the church hall she was the easiest to imagine as a drunk. She had what my father used to call 'a whisky voice', though she hadn't touched a drop for 15 years. 'I behaved in a very unladylike fashion,' she recalled. 'And I don't know if you agree with me, but I think there's something particularly undignified about the sight of a drunk woman.'

This produced a sniffle of feminist disapproval from a couple of young women in the room, who looked like business executives: the meeting was hosted by one of the Wren churches in the City of London. But no one argued with Pippa's claim that she suffered from a disease. I attended those lunchtime meetings three times a week in the shaky few months after I stopped drinking, and never once did I hear alcoholism described as anything other than a physical illness. 'Allergy' was one description; much more common was the phrase borrowed from the 'Big Book', the bible of Alcoholics Anonymous – 'a cunning, baffling and powerful disease'.

I had no doubt that I was an alcoholic. Alcoholism is the name for addiction to alcohol, and therefore I was also an addict – a useful word to describe someone who indulges in a pursuit so excessively that it harms them. The AA fellowship kept me away from alcohol thanks to the remarkable power of peer-group moral support, and especially the support of strangers, which has its own special potency. But I never thought my alcoholism, or any form of addiction, was a disease. Wisely, though, I kept that opinion to myself at those lunchtime meetings.

Lots of the attendees, Pippa included, seemed almost proud they had this 'disease'. They talked about it in the defensive but boastful manner in which, years later, people would discuss their recently discovered 'food intolerances'. They also referred all the time to 'the alcoholic personality', as if everyone who ended up in the rooms shared deeply rooted personality traits. Again, I couldn't see it: on the contrary, I was surprised by how little the members of the fellowship had in common. But if I'd questioned any aspect of the AA worldview, I'd have been corrected immediately: 'Don't you dare tell *me* I haven't got a disease!' Or I'd have been fobbed off with words of wisdom: 'Alcoholism is the one disease that tells you that you haven't got it' – an infuriating AA epigram designed to close down debate rather than open it up.

IS ADDICTION REALLY A 'DISEASE'?

Alcoholics Anonymous dates its foundation from 1935, when it changed from a specifically Christian mission to drunks into an independent fellowship of self-help groups with a strong but deliberately all-inclusive religious ethos. Since then, AA has achieved two extraordinary things. First, it has saved the lives of innumerable drunks. I'm probably one of them, so I feel a bit churlish suggesting that its other major achievement – the dissemination of the disease model – has distorted the modern world's understanding of addiction.

The fellowship's first medical adviser, the psychiatrist Dr William Duncan Stillworth, declared: 'Alcoholism is not just a vice or a habit. This is a compulsion, this is pathological craving, this is *disease!*'[1]

This disease is both incurable and progressive, according to AA. The only way to keep its symptoms under control is by a programme of total abstinence based on the famous 12 steps to recovery. In Step 1, sufferers acknowledge their powerlessness over alcohol. Other steps tell them to seek help from God, examine their character defects and make amends for the harm they caused when they were drinking. But – and this is the crucial point – AA reassures them that they cannot be blamed for the wreckage of their lives, because the disease robbed them of their free will.

This raises an obvious question. What about heavy drinkers who give up alcohol of their own accord, without any help from AA or the steps? The fellowship's answer is a masterpiece of circular logic. Since these drunks exercised free will in stopping drinking, and since the disease of addiction robs you of your free will, they cannot have had the disease and were therefore never alcoholics in the first place.

That AA formula has had an extraordinary appeal for generations of ex-drinkers. The organisation has 1.2 million members in the United States who attend 55,000 meeting groups; there are over two million members worldwide. The fellowship is sometimes described as a religious movement, but it would be more accurate to describe it as a self-help group with religious overtones. The Big Book talks explicitly about God, though it adds that 'God' is shorthand for 'a power greater than yourself'. That power can be a supernatural being or (for atheists and agnostics) simply the fellowship itself.

The disease model, enshrined in the 12 steps, has spread everywhere, perhaps thanks to the fact that AA has never attempted to copyright it. It's happy for anyone to borrow its formula. As Brendan Koerner put it in *Wired* magazine, the 12 steps became 'essentially open source code that anyone was free to build on, adding whatever features they wished'.[2]

As a result, there are around 200 separate 12-step fellowship networks covering all sorts of addictions. Narcotics Anonymous and Gamblers Anonymous have flourished since the 1950s, Overeaters Anonymous since 1960. Marijuana, cocaine, crystal meth and nicotine have their own 12-step programmes. (In Nicotine Anonymous, being tobacco-free is referred to as being 'smober'.) There are fellowships dedicated to sex addiction and co-dependence. Online Gamers Anonymous was founded in 2002.

IS ADDICTION REALLY A 'DISEASE'?

These groups have their own take on the 12 steps, but they leave intact the part of the open-source code that identifies addiction as a disease. Indeed, the vast majority of professional addiction specialists also embrace it. When Alcoholics Anonymous tells its members that medical opinion overwhelmingly thinks of addiction as a disease, it is telling the truth.

But that doesn't mean that medical opinion is right. On closer examination, many specialists derive their ideas from 12-step groups rather than the other way round. Let me illustrate why I think the disease model is flawed by telling the stories of two addicts who were friends of mine.

•

In the late 1990s I got to know two young men, Robin and James, who had been inseparable at university. They were in their late 20s, bright, charming and socially ambitious. Both had been to minor public schools but neither had got into Oxford or Cambridge, so when they arrived at their redbrick university they had to settle for its wannabe *Brideshead* drinking societies. At least once a fortnight they would dress up in black tie and perform the charming party tricks they associated with Oxbridge – climbing up scaffolding and urinating on pedestrians, that sort of thing. When their hangovers allowed, they read Evelyn Waugh, whose cruel snobbery delighted them. They were less keen on textbooks and, despite fluent pens, did badly in exams.

After university they drifted from one undemanding job to another, in the process spending more and more time in the company of ex-public school wasters who used hard drugs. Neither Robin nor James was especially rich, but both had just enough private money to feed their dealers. Eventually they replaced their office jobs with 'freelance' occupations that didn't require raising their heads from the pillow until the first of the afternoon soap operas. Both sets of parents were in despair, and raided their savings to pay for expensive spells in rehab that achieved nothing.

By 2000 the two men were boringly obsessed with getting high on any psychotropic substance they could lay their hands on, ranging from heroin to painkillers. At around that time I had a wisdom tooth taken out in the dentist's chair and was given a supply of dihydrocodeine tablets that I didn't take because they made me nauseous. I mentioned this to James, and within half an hour Robin was on the phone. 'I hear you've got some DF118s,' he said. I checked the label. Yes, that was what it said. 'Since they make you puke, why not let me take them off your hands?' he asked.

Robin and James were, or seemed to be, the most irredeemable addicts I've ever met. I was relieved when they drifted out of my life. I once caught sight of James hovering around the wines and spirits section of a supermarket in Bristol: this was the heyday of dirt-cheap own-brand vodka, and judging by the contents of his trolley he was taking full advantage of the special offers.

And now, five years later? Robin has a steady girlfriend, a baby daughter and a job in social media that has enabled him to start paying off his mortgage. He and his family are about to move to San Francisco, where he will work for an internet start-up. He gave up drink and drugs slowly, cutting out one substance after another, without relying on the 12 steps for guidance. 'They just remind me of the bad old days in rehab,' he explains. 'My home-made recovery was a long and messy business, with plenty of false starts, but it did work in the end.'

James is dead. He killed himself by jumping from the fifth floor of an apartment block in Johannesburg in 2006. It seems to have been a spur-of-the-moment thing, but who knows? He didn't leave a suicide note.

How can we explain the difference in the fates of the two friends? The 12-step explanation would be that Robin was never a real alcoholic or addict, since he cured himself without following the principles of the programme. He did attend AA and NA meetings, both in and out of clinics, but found them useless. 'AA members kept regaling me with these over-polished anecdotes about their miraculous recoveries, while the NA meetings seemed to be full of people who'd been clean for a couple of days and were obviously hoping to score.'

James, in contrast, met the sort of grisly fate that, according to the Big Book, awaits most untreated addicts. In the eyes of the fellowship, his leap from the balcony proved that he was the genuine article. One of the least attractive characteristics of 12-step 'old-timers' is the relish with which they describe disasters that befall those who stray from the true path.

But suppose that Robin and James had died at the same time, at the height of their drinking and drug-taking. (Robin did nearly kill himself with an accidental overdose, so it's not an unlikely scenario.) Would a post-mortem on their brains have been able to establish which of them had the 'progressive disease' of addiction and which was just going through a phase? The answer is no.

Moreover, if Robin and James had been subjected to a battery of tests when they were still alive, it's extremely unlikely that any of those tests would have distinguished between the 'real' alcoholic, doomed without 12-step treatment, from the 'fake' or temporary one, capable of curing himself. My guess is that the doctors would have said, correctly: both these young men are addicted to alcohol and drugs. But if the doctors were 12-step believers, as so many are, they might have added that neither of them could cure himself. Robin would have proved them wrong.

●

If you doubt that addiction medicine is heavily flavoured by 12-step dogma, let me point you in the direction of one of the most recent, supposedly authoritative, definitions of addiction by doctors specialising in the subject. It was published in 2011 by the American Society of Addiction Medicine (ASAM), which represents physicians who work with chemically dependent patients.

'Addiction is a primary, chronic disease of brain reward, motivation, memory and related circuitry,' it declares. 'Dysfunction in these circuits leads to characteristic biological, psychological, social and spiritual manifestations. This is reflected in an individual pathologically pursuing reward and/or relief by substance use and other behaviours.

'Addiction is characterised by inability to consistently abstain, impairment in behavioural control, craving, diminished recognition of significant problems with one's behaviours and interpersonal relationships, and a dysfunctional emotional response.

'Like other chronic diseases, addiction often involves cycles of relapse and remission. Without treatment or engagement in recovery activities, addiction is progressive and can result in disability or premature death.'[3]

This is what a definition looks like when it has been drafted by a committee. The 80 doctors who worked on it seem to have thrown everything at it but the kitchen sink. But what their definition cannot conceal – indeed, what it inadvertently reveals – is that addiction is far too complex a phenomenon for doctors to classify as a disease in the sense that cancer and tuberculosis are diseases. Hence the waffle.

Addiction specialists wouldn't tie themselves in such knots if they had a diagnostic test for the 'disease' of addiction. But there is no such test.

Not only is addiction unlike cancer and diabetes, which show up in lab results. It's also unlike brain diseases such as Alzheimer's. That, too, lacks a simple diagnostic test: in its early stages its symptoms can be mistaken for stress or other forms of dementia. But eventually the *involuntary* behaviour of the patient should allow the doctor to make an accurate diagnosis, after which its progress is truly inevitable. There is no 12-step programme for Alzheimer's to keep its symptoms under control. The end point is death, after which an autopsy will probably reveal shrinking of the brain that provides final confirmation of the diagnosis.

I'm not saying that medicine can't identify addiction in the ordinary sense of the word: of course it can. Scientists can test for chemical dependence on a drug. They can measure a patient's tolerance for it and predict the withdrawal symptoms. They can identify the precise damage caused by substance abuse and hazard a guess as to life expectancy. They can look at a patient and say: this person is an addict.

But what they can't tell, even with brain-scanning technology, is whether a neurochemical 'switch' has been thrown which induces *irreversible* addiction, which is what disease-model advocates are now suggesting. We don't even know whether such a switch exists. It's a fashionable theory, but that's all it is.

Post-mortems can't identify a disease of addiction, either. A dead body may reveal organ damage caused by taking a particular drug, but it won't necessarily tell doctors much about the behaviour that accompanied it. You can't know from looking at the liver of someone who drank themselves to death whether their drinking followed classic addictive patterns. People develop fatal cirrhosis of the liver – a proper disease by any definition – from regular wine consumption that isn't compulsive in character. Non-alcoholics in France die from this sort of drinking all the time. Likewise, the body of an obese person won't tell you whether they ate addictively. Their obesity may have been caused by an illness that stopped them exercising, for example.

Why, then, is the ASAM definition of addiction so confident in its claim that addiction is a 'primary, chronic disease' – an assertion that it proceeds to justify with woolly and overlapping generalisations?

At the risk of sounding like a conspiracy theorist, I think the answer lies in the role of 12-step groups in devising the treatment programmes run by the doctors in ASAM.

There's a bit of a giveaway in the definition. This says that dysfunction in the brain's rewards circuits leads to characteristic 'spiritual manifestations'. I've heard that phrase before. During my AA years, as I sat drinking powdered coffee in draughty basements, it was drummed into me that alcoholism was a *spiritual* disease. That is Big Book teaching; you hear it in virtually every meeting. But if you're trying to define addiction, you run up against a problem: there is no agreed methodology for measuring 'spiritual manifestations'. How could there be? In all my years spent studying the sociology of religion, I never came across an agreed definition of 'spirituality'. It's just the sort of concept that scholars fight over.

Many addiction specialists have a habit of throwing around words as if everyone agreed on their meaning. They'll use a term like 'compulsion' without exploring the philosophical questions it raises about free will. They wander into other disciplines – philosophy, sociology and theology – without seeming to realise they're doing so. Nothing must be allowed to challenge the one-size-fits-all model of the 12 steps.[4]

According to the psychologist Dr Stanton Peele, a long-standing critic of disease-centred definitions of addiction, 'the American Society of Addiction Medicine was created – and is dominated – by true-believer 12-step types'.[5] Peele argues that AA preserved the temperance movement's message of total abstinence – deeply rooted in American Protestant society – while relieving guilt by naming illness rather than sin as the cause of addiction. Also, 12-step advocates have proved to be expert lobbyists, persuading health institutes that theirs is the only recovery programme that works, and influencing judges and magistrates to send criminals on compulsory 12-step courses. Most substance abuse treatment in the US is based on 12-step models.[6]

Unfortunately, the media rarely bother to question the assumptions and allegiances that lie behind the pronouncements of addiction specialists. 'Addiction is a brain disease, experts declare,' said the *LA Times* when ASAM published its definition. 'Addiction a brain disorder, not just bad behaviour,' said *USA Today*.

But the most enthusiastic coverage came from *The Fix* (no relation to this book), an upmarket website aimed at recovering addicts with disposable incomes. It declared: 'If you think addiction is all about booze, drugs, sex, gambling, food and other irresistible vices, think again. And if you believe that a person has a choice whether or not to indulge in an addictive behaviour, get over it.' ASAM had blown the whistle on these notions, said *The Fix*, by revealing addiction to be a fundamental impairment in the experience of pleasure that 'literally compels' the addict to chase the chemical highs produced by drugs, sex, food and gambling.[7]

Note the finger-wagging tone of the article. If you think choice is involved in addictive behaviour, 'get over it'. I can imagine Pippa nodding her head vigorously at that. When I showed the article to Robin, the former alcohol and heroin addict, he smiled and said: 'That's exactly the sort of take-it-or-leave-it message I heard every day when I was in treatment.'

Robin was in a rehab unit run by the Priory, a fashionable and expensive healthcare provider which specialises in alcohol and drug treatment and is best known for its celebrity alumni, who include Kate Moss, Robbie Williams, Courtney Love, Pete Doherty and the late Amy Winehouse. (As that list suggests, its track record is patchy at best.) Robin told me about his experience of the treatment there.

When I was in the Priory, all the doctors and counsellors emphasised the disease concept. We had lectures in the afternoons. One was from the medical director, a psychiatrist, on the disease concept. You have a disease, the disease of addiction, 'dis-ease', etc. When I asked him for the evidence, he said things like 'we can see that the metabolic pathways are different in alcoholics'. Well of course they are, because the booze, not the 'disease', has changed them. I didn't think he was being very intellectually honest, but he was the expert and if we had different ideas that was just evidence of the alcoholic's arrogance.

As for the counsellors, they kept talking about 'the illness'. Your illness, my illness. 'My illness tells me I'm a bad person.' The reason for this emphasis was that 'it's a shame-based illness', and the whole point is to get away from the idea that you've been a wicked person and you should be ashamed – such 'stinking thinking' might cause you to fall into a 'shame spiral', and shame leads you to 'pick up' the next drink or drug.

You'd absorb the illness chat pretty quickly, but I could never bring myself to talk in terms of 'my illness' – it just seemed too pat and convenient to take away responsibility and turn your addiction into something outside yourself.

Addiction specialists would reply that of course they're not saying the disease is 'outside' people. But the way they talk about addicts sometimes implies that sufferers are under the control of a malign puppetmaster.

There are recognised brain diseases which, like addiction, manifest themselves as behaviour – the jerking limbs of Huntingdon's, for example. But it's a funny sort of primary, chronic, brain disorder that makes you drive yourself to the pub, sink seven pints of beer with whisky chasers, and then drive yourself back, turning your car into a weapon of mass destruction.

In fact, there's a world of difference between involuntary, chaotic spasms and long sequences of actions that look perfectly voluntary, if misguided, to anyone observing them. Professor John Booth Davies, director of the Centre for Applied Social Psychology at the University of Strathclyde – and one of Britain's most prominent opponents of the disease model – makes the point that if a disease can force people to steal, to lift up glasses, or to stick needles in their arms when they're actually trying not to, then any goal-directed behaviour could be a symptom of disease.[8]

The behaviour of addicts looks voluntary because it is. However intense the temptations offered by substances and experiences, there will always be people who, having given in to them, change their mind and pull themselves out of addiction.

As we've seen, AA brushes aside this phenomenon with unbreakable circular logic: if you cure yourself, you were never an addict. Medically qualified addiction specialists basically agree, though they usually espouse a more nuanced version of the disease theory. They don't deny that some addicts appear to cure themselves – but they treat such cases as outliers or questionable diagnoses. The official line remains that, to quote the *Sourcebook on Substance Abuse*, 'the majority of individuals who receive treatment for substance abuse relapse'.[9] Clinical reports that between 50 and 60 per cent of patients relapse within six months of ending treatment are accepted as evidence of the power of the disease.

There's something wrong with this methodology, however, as Gene M. Heyman, a hospital research psychologist and lecturer at Harvard University, points out.

'Most research is based on addicts who come to clinics,' he says. 'But these are a distinct minority, and they are much more likely to keep using drugs past the age of 30 – probably because they have many more health problems than non-clinic addicts. They are about twice as likely to suffer from depression, and are many times more likely to have HIV/AIDS. These problems interfere with activities that can successfully compete with drug use. Thus, experts have based their view of addiction on an unrepresentative sample of addicts.'[10]

Heyman went looking for large-scale studies of addiction in the US based on more representative samples of addicts in the general population, not just in clinics. He found four of them, carried out by leading researchers and funded by national health institutes.[11] Yet, mysteriously, the clinical texts and journal articles spreading the message of a 'primary, chronic, relapsing disease' fail to mention these epidemiological studies. Why?

Could it have been because none of the surveys found that most addicts eventually relapse? What they suggested, inconveniently, was that between 60 and 80 per cent of individuals who met the criteria for lifetime addiction stopped using drugs in their late twenties or early thirties. In short, high remission rates would seem to be a stable feature of addiction.[12]

●

In 1970 there was a shockingly sudden burst of heroin addiction among GIs in Vietnam. As Alfred McCoy describes in his book *The Politics of Heroin*, until 1969 the 'Golden Triangle' of south-east Asia was harvesting nearly a thousand tons of raw opium annually – but there were no laboratories capable of turning it into high-grade heroin. That changed when Chinese master chemists from Hong Kong arrived in the region. Suddenly South Vietnam was full of fine-grained No. 4 heroin instead of the impure, chunky No. 3 grade.

'Heroin addiction spread like the plague,' writes McCoy. 'Fourteen-year-old girls were selling heroin at roadside stands on the main highway from Saigon to the US army base at Long Binh; Saigon street peddlers stuffed plastic vials of 95 percent pure heroin into the pockets of GIs as they strolled through downtown Saigon; and "mama-sans", or Vietnamese barracks' maids, started carrying a few vials to work for sale to on-duty GIs.'[13]

By the summer of 1970, virtually every enlisted man in Vietnam was being offered high-quality heroin. Almost half of them took it at least once; between 15 and 20 per cent of GIs in the Mekong delta were snorting heroin or smoking cigarettes laced with it. Ironically, heroin use soared after the Army cracked down on the much more easily detectable habit of smoking pungent marijuana. But the key factor, argues McCoy, is that drug manufacturers could make $88 million a year from selling heroin to soldiers; no wonder that 'base after base was overrun by these ant-armies of heroin pushers with their identical plastic vials'. Rumours spread that the North Vietnamese were behind this intense marketing campaign – what better way to immobilise the enemy? But the truth was that South Vietnamese government officials were protecting the pushers.

In any case, combat troops avoided heroin use in the field: being stoned, especially on a drug as soporific as heroin, was more likely to get them killed. But they made up for it when they returned to base. One soldier came back from a long patrol of 13 days; his first action was to tip a vial of heroin into a shot of vodka and knock it back.[14]

Panicky headlines about the 'GI epidemic' started appearing in American newspapers. The Nixon administration was terrified of a crime wave caused by the return of thousands of desperate junkies to American cities. But it never materialised. Instead, the addicted soldiers cleaned up their act – fast.

We know this because the US government, anticipating disaster, commissioned a medical study that recruited more than 400 returning soldiers who snorted, smoked or injected heroin *and* described themselves as addicted (making it possibly the largest ever study of heroin users). To researchers' surprise, back in the United States only 12 per cent of these addicts carried on using heroin at a level that met the study's criteria for addiction.[15]

This is really powerful evidence that changes in social environment can dramatically affect people's drug-taking habits. As Professor Michael Gossop, a leading researcher at the National Addiction Centre, King's College, London, explains: 'The young men who served in Vietnam were removed from their normal social environment and from many of its usual social and moral constraints. For many of them it was a confusing, chaotic and often extremely frightening experience and the chances of physical escape were remote except through the hazardous possibilities of self-inflicted injury.'[16] Gossop uses the phrase 'inward desertion' to describe what heroin offered the soldiers: a cheap trip to another world.

The scared, disorientated soldiers in Vietnam were being offered a chemical fix to relieve their fear. The social and psychological pressure to do something they would never dream of doing in America – take heroin – was intense: one in five slid all the way into addiction. But, once home again, they weren't scared any more. They weren't mixing with other users. The drug was expensive, hard to find, low-grade and highly illegal. The pressure went into reverse. In other words, the same combination of social and psychological factors that turned these men into addicts explains why they were able to stop.

True, these were remarkable circumstances. So we might expect other addicts, whose initiation into drug use was less dramatic and more gradual, to recover at a slower rate. And that's precisely what those four big epidemiological studies show: they paint a picture of users slowly changing their behaviour when their circumstances changed. They don't support the progressive disease model. The Vietnam statistics, meanwhile, directly undermine it. The US government went to a lot of trouble to make sure that the soldiers it was testing were addicts. Are we supposed to believe that the 88 per cent who later kicked the habit were misdiagnosed? Or that being drafted to fight in heroin-saturated Vietnam 'doesn't count' because it was such an unusual situation?

The Vietnam survey identifies a key factor in addiction: availability. To quote Michael Gossop: 'Availability is such an obvious determinant of drug taking that it is often overlooked. In its simplest form the availability hypothesis states that *the greater the availability of a drug in a society, the more people are likely to use it and the more they are likely to run into problems with it* [my italics].'[17]

This hypothesis might seem like a statement of the obvious. Actually, as Gossop says, the question of availability is often treated as a secondary factor, less important than any predisposition to a so-called 'disease'.

Gossop identifies different dimensions of availability. There's physical availability, obviously, but also psychological availability (whether someone's personality, background and beliefs increases their interest in using particular drugs), economic availability (whether the drugs are affordable) and social availability (whether the social context encourages use of the drugs). In the case of Vietnam, he points out, many soldiers found that all the boxes were ticked. Troops in Thailand, by contrast, could easily get hold of heroin – but their lives were not in danger, they were free to move among a friendly population and their peers were not using it. Less than one per cent of military personnel took the drug.[18]

Availability doesn't offer a comprehensive explanation for addiction, but it reminds us that we cannot hope to understand why people engage in addictive activities – be it shooting up heroin in the jungle or gorging on muffins in Starbucks – unless we take account of what that activity means in its social setting.

No one who has watched *The Wire*, the magnificent television epic of life in drug-saturated districts of Baltimore, can seriously propose that it depicts a black population afflicted by chronic disease. The characters in the show who smoke heroin do so, basically, because they live in districts where everyone does. If I lived there, I'd be a smack addict. Since I'm an addict, perhaps that goes without saying. But I have a sneaking feeling that even my local vicar would be hooked on the stuff.

Gossop, who has advised the British government on drug policy, is unusual among addiction experts for the bluntness with which he dismisses the disease theory. He describes addiction as a 'habit'. That may sound less scary than an irreversible disease, but it isn't. In a society overflowing with abundance, the implications of a habit of addiction driven by availability are every bit as alarming as those of a disease that strikes only individuals with malfunctioning brains.

This isn't to deny that some people are naturally more vulnerable to addiction than others. And we can't ignore recent discoveries in neuroscience, which show how the brain's natural reward systems are being hijacked by newly available substances and gadgets. In the next chapter, we'll look at what the brain does and doesn't tell us about addiction.

But I want to end this chapter by stressing, yet again, the inadequacies of the disease model. If the word 'disease' is at all useful in this context, it's as a metaphor for addiction, not as a diagnosis. And I can think of another vivid metaphor that works just as well. Modern consumers are like soldiers drafted to Vietnam – disorientated, fearful and relentlessly tempted by fixes that promise to make reality more bearable. You don't have to be ill to give in; just human.

3
WHAT THE BRAIN TELLS US (AND WHAT IT DOESN'T)

Imagine the embarrassment. You are a retired civil servant with Parkinson's disease. You are industrious and introverted, like many sufferers from the condition. (We don't know for sure why it often strikes people with this type of personality, but the correlation was noted as long ago as the 19th century.[1]) You're a regular at your local pub, where you're known as a modest, affable chap who orders half-pints rather than pints. Occasionally you while away 20 minutes by pushing a few coins into the slot machine, accepting your losses with a philosophical shrug.

Then something odd happens. Without warning, you develop an obsession with playing the machine. You stand in front of it from opening time until last orders, much to the bemusement of the other regulars. You know that the pub's fruit machine is programmed to return only 80 per cent of the money you put into it, but one day you hit multiple jackpots that earn you £50. The thrill of this experience – and the possibility of it happening again

– reinforces your new preoccupation. You are no longer thinking rationally.

Eventually the teasing from other patrons turns to alarm as they see you pouring away your pension. The pub landlord has 'a quiet word' and asks you to stop playing. You're mortified and stop going to the pub – but, instead of finding another place to drink, you slip into your local betting shop, where the jackpots are bigger. Then a newspaper article about online gambling catches your eye and before long you are shutting yourself away in your study, steadily building up credit card bills as you accrue greater and greater losses. Your wife still doesn't have a clue.

But your problems don't end there. Somewhere along the line, much to your own surprise, you discover a taste for internet pornography. Under normal circumstances, porn would have no appeal – you're 70 years old, after all. But even before you stumbled across these sites you had noticed that your sexual appetite had mysteriously reawakened.

This story sounds implausible, but something very much like it happened to several Parkinson's patients recently. They developed gambling urges out of nowhere, and in certain cases these were accompanied by a revived sex drive. There were other permutations: patients experienced a revved-up sex drive without the gambling urges, or started binge eating. Some began shopping obsessively, perhaps combining it with other risk-taking activities. The common thread was the startling change in the behaviour of people who, until recently, had devoted most of their leisure time to tending their begonias.

But the culprit wasn't the disease. It was the medication designed to reverse its symptoms. The medicine wasn't supposed to produce those results, but the fact that it did so provides us with vital information about the strange, self-defeating behaviours that we call addictions.

•

These Parkinson's patients had been given drugs that mimicked the action of dopamine. This is a neurotransmitter, or chemical messenger, that affects our experience of pleasure and also has the ability to map out new reward pathways in the brain – in other words, to rewire it.

That's a trendy way of describing complex changes in the brain. This is arguably the most impenetrable subject human beings have ever tried to understand. Scientists who have devoted their careers to it admit that they have only pieced together a tiny section of the jigsaw. That's frustrating – but bear with me, because what they have discovered has fascinating implications. Dopamine is an ancient mechanism: it's found in lizards and every other animal along the evolutionary tree. It has been called the 'pleasure chemical' because it is released whenever we eat good food, enjoy sex or take pleasure-enhancing drugs.

Recently, scientists have refined their understanding of dopamine. They now think that it has more to do with desire than pleasure – or, to use the refreshingly simple terms that now loom large in scientific discussions of addiction, with *wanting* rather than *liking*.

WHAT THE BRAIN TELLS US (AND WHAT IT DOESN'T)

In a series of experiments on the brains of rats, the psychologist Kent Berridge of the University of Michigan came to the conclusion that 'wanting' (desire) and 'liking' (pleasure) are separate urges controlled by different brain circuits in humans as well as animals. That is an important discovery that we need to keep at the back of our minds whenever we think about how and why we are behaving addictively.

Dopamine is involved in both brain circuits, but its main function is to stimulate wanting; liking is more affected by the opioid system, which contains endorphins, the brain's natural morphine-like compounds.[2] Of the two urges, wanting is more powerful. 'The brain seems to be more stingy with mechanisms for pleasure than for desire,' says Berridge.[3]

This helps us understand another apparently simple distinction made by scientists that we came across in Chapter 1 – between the Stop and Go impulses in the brain. The Go impulse tells us to reach out for an immediate reward; it's ancient, it's powerful and it's shared with animals. As you might expect, it goes into overdrive at the prospect of food and sex. Dopamine and 'wanting' are central to this urge – but different levels of 'liking' also determine the strength of the Go message.[4]

The Stop impulse is highly developed only in humans. It helps us manage our Go impulse by spelling out the consequences of immediate reward. You could call it the voice of reason; it comes from the frontal lobes of the human brain. These are not fully developed in adolescents, who are therefore poor at managing the Stop impulse. This will not come as a surprise to the parents of teenage children.

Let's return to the traumatic experience of those Parkinson's patients. Their disease drains the brain of dopamine. Indeed, it may begin to do so decades before more obvious symptoms become apparent. That could explain why Parkinson's seems to disproportionately affect people with introverted personalities: those self-effacing traits may not be signs of natural, life-long introversion but, rather, the first symptoms of the disease, appearing years before diagnosis.

The patients who developed sudden gambling or other impulsive habits had been given dopamine agonists, which, by boosting dopamine, usually slow down the progression of the disease. They are a common treatment and can be remarkably effective. An aunt of mine with Parkinson's was given one of these drugs. The brightening of her personality and her fresh pleasure in everyday experiences, such as looking at her garden, seemed almost miraculous. For some patients, however, the same chemical that restored my aunt's *joie de vivre* was psychological poison.

Alan Burrows, a pensioner from Queensland, was one of 100 Australians who sued the drug company Pfizer after taking its dopamine agonist medication Cabaser. He claims that it caused him to start binge gambling on 'pokies' (Australian slang for slot machines). Eventually, he had to sell his house to pay off his $300,000 gambling debts. 'Once I started I had to keep going, by withdrawing money every hour, until I couldn't get any more money,' he said. 'It was a compulsion to do it. You became really devious, disgusting.'[5]

WHAT THE BRAIN TELLS US (AND WHAT IT DOESN'T)

It's probably no consolation to Mr Burrows, but what happened to him and to the other Parkinson's sufferers who developed compulsive habits helps us to draw the boundaries of addiction. Their ordeal suggests that dopamine is a common factor in habits that society has been slow to label 'addictions' because they don't involve drugs.

After the stories of bad reactions to Parkinson's drugs surfaced, Dr Valerie Voon of the US National Institutes of Health led a study of patients given dopamine agonists. She found that 13 per cent exhibited 'a constellation of pathological behaviours, including gambling, shopping, binge eating and hypersexuality'.[6] They did so because they were being over-supplied with dopamine.

The inference we can draw from this is valuable. It seems that people who don't have Parkinson's disease but engage in the same pathological habits are also having problems with their dopamine levels. Gambling, obsessive shopping, binge eating, hypersexuality – note how those Parkinson's patients found themselves caught up in the sort of activities where wanting overwhelms liking. Also, they were being driven by *repetitive* urges. This is typical of dopamine at work, laying down new patterns in the brain as it takes effect. As the psychiatrist Norman Doidge explains: 'The same surge of dopamine that thrills us also consolidates the neuronal connections responsible for the behaviours that led us to accomplish our goal.'[7]

In other words, the more we experience dopamine-induced pleasure, the more we want to repeat the experience. But, thanks to levels of tolerance that have been raised by rewiring, the harder we have to work to repeat it to our satisfaction. That is why addicts always seem to be looking for a bigger and bigger hit.

All substance abusers experience surges of dopamine, often accompanied by craving – that is, very strong feelings of wanting. Alcohol, amphetamine, cocaine, heroin, marijuana and nicotine all increase the supply of dopamine to the nucleus accumbens, a pleasure centre buried deep in the brain that has been called the final destination of the reward pathway.[8]

This does *not* mean that addicts are people born with naturally high or low levels of dopamine, nor that they have inherited cravings that force them to keep stimulating the rush of dopamine into their nucleus accumbens. If any of these things could be proved, then the study of addiction science wouldn't involve so much infuriating guesswork.

Different recreational drugs do different things to the brain. They produce different rewards – and different punishments. You don't have to take them to know that; you just have to observe the behaviour of their users. It's a bit like visiting the zoo.

Coke-heads and speed freaks gabble excitedly as they are swept along on a tide of dopamine. When that tide pulls out, they experience a particular sort of come-down. 'Coke is the drug we save for the time after we get back from clubbing,' says Olly, 27, a graphic designer. 'It runs out pretty quickly. Presuming we don't order more, by 4 a.m. everyone is getting jittery and anxious. You see people's eyes flicking around the room wondering if anyone's got any left. A group of four chatty and gobby friends suddenly becomes four individuals chewing the insides of their cheeks. The next morning we go for brunch to cure our hangovers but everyone's coming down off the coke, snapping at each other. Some people feel blue for days.'

Heroin users don't inflict logorrhea on their friends: their drug is forcing the brain to over-produce endorphins, those natural euphoria-inducing and painkilling neurotransmitters. Heroin suppresses neuro-transmission in the central nervous system, which can produce an exquisitely calm feeling, particularly if your nerves were shot to pieces in the first place. This can take people to the gates of paradise, but also to hell: the come-down is long and usually profoundly depressing, because the nucleus accumbens is extremely sensitive to opioid withdrawal.[9]

Also, the brain's self-regulatory process means that junkies quickly need to increase their doses to slow down neurotransmission; in severe cases, they inject themselves hourly in order to maintain a state of mental paralysis. William Burroughs, writing about his last year of addiction in North Africa, said he could look at the end of his shoe for eight hours. And if a friend had visited him and died on the spot, 'I would have sat there looking at my shoe waiting to go through his pockets.'[10]

Ecstasy releases serotonin, a neurotransmitter associated with happiness; hence its users' indiscriminate declarations of affection. 'One of the reasons I don't do pills is seeing how fucking annoying people are when they're "loved up"', says Ollie. 'MDMA [a purer form of Ecstasy] is even worse. You see groups of heterosexual men hugging and kissing each other. There's this idiotic bear hugging that goes on for hours, and I'm afraid it makes me laugh when I see them at work on Monday, looking sheepish and sad.' The sheepishness is self-explanatory; the sadness is pure dopamine deprivation.

Alcohol, meanwhile, has been called the most ruthless of all brain-hijackers. Looking back on my drinking, I now have some idea of what was happening to my body; I just wish I'd known at the time, if only to avoid some hangovers of apocalyptic proportions.

Alcohol molecules are quite unlike those of other addicting drugs. They have the ability to speed up the transmission of chemicals that excite us and also, later, those that relax us, sometimes to the point of stupor. We're talking about a fiendishly complicated neurochemical dance that releases inhibitions and twists moods over the course of an evening. I reckon my own dopamine would peak around the third glass of red wine, which was the moment when – if I was on form – I was most fun to be around. By the third bottle the flow of mood-enhancing chemicals would have slowed down and the inhibitory neurotransmitter GABA would be in the ascendant. My voice would become slurred and my thoughts confused – but I'd be chasing the vanishing high by drinking even faster. And my friends, sensibly, would have made their excuses and left.

As for the hangovers – well, if ever I feel like going back on the sauce after 18 years I have only to cast my mind back to any of the thousand or so I inflicted on myself. Perhaps it was the ability of the alcohol molecule to insinuate itself into so many different functions of the brain that produced such all-encompassing misery. But, as we'll see later, I eventually discovered an effective but fabulously stupid pharmaceutical remedy for those feelings.

All intoxicating experiences involve a cocktail of brain chemicals that are mixed quite differently depending on the nature of the behaviour. But dopamine is still the master drug that, in the words of the research psychiatrist Morten Kringelbach, 'appears to encode desire' and can make us chase after something long after we've ceased to derive much pleasure from it.[11] To quote Dirk Hansen, 'dopamine is part of the reason why we remember how much we liked getting high yesterday'.[12]

As this suggests, it's good at fastening on to cues. One sensible piece of advice that 12-step groups dole out to their members is to avoid 'people, places and things' that were part of their old habits. 'If you hang around barbers' shops, sooner or later you're going to get a haircut,' is an AA saying – meaning, of course, that sitting around drinking orange juice in the pub is risky for an alcoholic. The more addicted you become to something, the more sensitive you become to these cues – even after years of abstinence. Significantly, these cues are often the 'things' that have come to replace people in your life.

But the link between cues and desire isn't confined to addicts. It's part of everyday existence for people situated all along the addictive spectrum – that is, all human beings.

You don't need to ingest any substance at all to experience a rush of dopamine: the cue is enough. The smell or even just the sight of food increases dopamine in the nucleus accumbens, the region of the brain involved in reward and motivation. It's why our mouths water. As the psychology professors Harvey Milkman and Stanley Sunderwirth explain, this is the same type of neurochemical response that occurs when a cocaine addict sees a video of people snorting a fat line of white powder: 'The dopamine messenger impels the organism to action, an impulse that sheer willpower cannot easily overcome.'[13]

I know what they mean. For some reason, watching characters drink red wine on television is more tempting for me than seeing them do it in real life; it makes me long to nip to the supermarket for a bottle of Rioja. (I don't, I hasten to add.) Why this should be I don't know, but in AA meetings I quite often heard speakers complain of the same thing. Some people even 'had a slip', to use 12-step terminology, thanks to things they had seen on screen. Cues can be made more powerful by being detached from everyday networks. This is why many slips happen when alcoholics are on holiday, away from the company of people who know they have a problem, where the booze is presented in an exotic setting that somehow detoxifies it. One businessman I know found himself – to his own astonishment – accepting a rum and coke from a stewardess on a plane flight. 'We were so high up that it didn't seem to count,' he said. And thus ended the decade of abstinence of which he'd been so proud.

Milkman and Sunderwirth have produced a list of activities that boost dopamine in the nucleus accumbens. They are: crime, eating, gambling, risk-taking, sex … and hugging your loved ones. With the possible exception of hugging, there's an addiction (or, more accurately, a huge range of addictions) lurking in all of them.

What's useful about this list is that it reminds us that the brain's reward circuits don't necessarily distinguish between supposedly innocent and supposedly dangerous pursuits. Once 'wanting' is out of control, previously innocuous substances or experiences can become life-threatening. A heart attack brought on by an obsession with cheeseburgers can be just as fatal as a heroin overdose. And, these days, people do become obsessed with burgers – perhaps because they are chemically engineered to be almost as addictive as heroin.

To recap: both substance addictions and 'process' (non-substance) addictions are associated with dopamine-related disorders of brain reward. I'm not suggesting that this is a simple explanation for addiction; clearly it isn't. But it's useful. We now know that addictive behaviours are accompanied by physical changes in the brain – whether or not they involve drugs. Once we delve deeper into the subject, however, things get a little harder to understand. In fact, the experts don't understand them, because neuroscience is still in its infancy.

Here's a question that illustrates its limitations. What do young lovers have in common with coke-snorters?

The answer, according to Norman Doidge, is that they experience a similar high. Cocaine's special relationship with dopamine creates feelings of radiant optimism. Like love-struck couples, people on cocaine are 'filled with hopeful anticipation and are sensitive to anything that might give them pleasure – flowers and fresh air inspire them and a slight but thoughtful gesture makes them delight in all mankind'.[14]

In other words, falling in love activates many of the same chemical pathways as inserting a rolled-up £20 note into your nostril. That's amusing to know – but it also gives you some idea of how difficult it is to diagnose addiction merely by looking at someone's brain. One recent scientific paper suggests that studying 'normal' people going through an intense romantic episode may help us understand the pathological vulnerability of drug addicts.[15] That sounds intriguing – but it also smacks of desperation. Clearly, neuroscience isn't even close to being able to match minuscule variations in brain reward circuits to specific patterns of behaviour. And, so far as I can tell, no two neuroscientists draw the boundaries of 'addiction' in the same place.

We've seen that different drugs boost dopamine in different ways. But that information isn't as helpful as it sounds, because dopamine can't tell the difference between addictive substances and rewarding but non-addictive substances.[16] The brain doesn't recognise our culturally determined categories of legal and illegal drugs, or our neat distinctions between drugs and foods, or the difference between heroic and self-destructive risk-taking.

And, as if that wasn't complicated enough, many addicts transfer their allegiance from one habit to another. If, for example, the supply of heroin runs out in a particular city, addicts will switch to cocaine – even though the gratifications the two drugs provide are quite different and involve separate reward systems. This comorbidity, as it's known, is a puzzle to scientists.

It's no wonder, therefore, that neuroscientists can't read backwards from a map of the brain's neural pathways to the behaviour that shaped them. All they can say is that specific signs of brain damage may have been caused by a particular habit, which is a very different proposition.

Why does science have such a hard time getting to grips with the phenomenon of addiction? In a nutshell, because human brains, as opposed to animal ones, can instruct the body to perform an almost infinite number of *voluntary* (and therefore unpredictable) actions. And, contrary to the beliefs of disease-model advocates and the huge therapeutic industry, addictive behaviour is essentially voluntary. Addicts may be influenced by their disordered brain chemistry to make bad choices, but they are choices nonetheless.

●

'I really shouldn't.' When you hear those three words, uttered in a resigned but excited tone of voice, what image do they conjure up? I hear the voice of my long-dead grandmother, knowing that another helping of my mother's apple crumble wasn't going to help her lose weight and was against doctor's orders. She had heart disease. But my grandmother couldn't resist – or, rather, chose not to. (In her defence, I should point out that my mother's crumble was to die for.)

Puddings are high on the list of British I-really-shouldn't items. Pity the poor waiters who listen in on the same ritual exchange night after night:

'I'll just have coffee, thanks.'

'Me too.'

'Well, I don't know about you, but that tiramisu looks awfully good.'

'Ooh, it does …'

'Can we have one tiramisu with two – no, make that three spoons.'

These people aren't so much exchanging thoughts with each other as with themselves. What's going on in their brains?

The neuroscientist David Eagleman compares brains to representative democracies in which parties hold different opinions about the same issues: 'They are built of multiple, overlapping experts who weigh in and compete over different choices. As Walt Whitman correctly surmised, we are large and we harbour multitudes within us. And those multitudes are locked in chronic battle. There is an ongoing conversation among the different factions in your brain, each competing to control the single output channel of your behaviour.'[17]

In essence, this is a more sophisticated way of describing the Stop and Go mechanisms. Animals can't have these conversations with themselves. They lack a fully developed prefrontal cortex, the part of the human brain that allows us to analyse situations and make reasoned choices. When a mouse is fed a drug targeted at a particular dopamine receptor, it will go into a frenzy of cocaine consumption.[18] Something very similar happens in the parts of the human brain that we share with mice. But, however intense the craving that a drug addict experiences, the decision to take the drug involves uniquely human, rational functions.

To put it another way, humans don't respond to their 'animal instincts' in the way that animals do. Rather, when temptation appears, those ancient instincts are fed through higher-order cognitive processes. And it's those rational processes – the battle between Stop and Go – that tend to decide the outcome.

A cocaine addict has the mental capacity to decide not to give in to temptation; a mouse doesn't. Of course, it's likely that the addict will succumb, but only after rationalising his decision to do so. ('I really shouldn't, but …') We should therefore be very careful about using the world 'compulsive' as a synonym for 'overwhelming'. P.J. O'Rourke once wrote that there was no agreed etiquette for declining a line of coke because no one ever had – but that was in the early 1980s when, incredibly, cocaine was being touted as non-addictive.

It would be convenient if neuroscience enabled us to identify addicts, and potential addicts, by measuring their brain activity. It does not do so. On the contrary, recent research undermines the neat distinction between addicts and non-addicts that has become so central to the therapeutic industry. We have a very incomplete picture of the relationship between addictive behaviour and the brain's reward systems. What we do know about the action of dopamine suggests that 'normal' over-indulgence and addictive over-indulgence are closely related to each other – not something that the disease-obsessed therapeutic industry is prepared to admit.

The essence of that disorder is that people *choose* to do things that are not in their best interests. In doing so, they are choosing short-term over long-term rewards. Those are the I-really-shouldn't moments, and they come in all shapes and sizes – from the last cupcake in the box to the impulse purchase of virtual goods in a computer game. How much harm they do depends on the context, obviously. Life would be pretty grim if we never said to ourselves 'to hell with the consequences'. In fact, I feel uncomfortable in the company of lifelong teetotallers, as opposed to ex-drunks like me. And people who boast that they've never even tried a cigarette strike me as annoyingly self-righteous and risk-averse. Weren't they at least curious?

The individuals we call addicts are those who consistently seek damaging short-term rewards. They seem to have a strong 'wanting' pathway in the brain. To what extent they were born with this type of pathway is difficult to say. Alcoholism runs in families, but trying to draw the line between genetic predisposition and environmental conditioning is an impossible task. This wouldn't be the case if addiction really were an organic disease such as Huntingdon's: scientists would stand a chance of isolating the gene that caused it. But, since addiction consists of complex sequences of voluntary acts, such neurological reductionism is a waste of time.

As we've seen, however, neuroscience helps explain what is going on when we behave addictively, irrespective of whether we're addicts.

WHAT THE BRAIN TELLS US (AND WHAT IT DOESN'T)

The pleasures we reach out for flood our brains with dopamine, among other substances, and then drain it. Illegal drugs offer extreme examples of this phenomenon. Methamphetamine and crack cocaine, for example, induce cravings that almost anyone would find hard to resist. One of my friends, a distinguished conservative journalist, was on holiday with his wife in Jamaica in the early 1990s, when the crack epidemic in American cities was at its height. They were offered a crack pipe and thought, OK, just this once. 'It was utter bliss,' he recalls. 'But my wife and I took a solemn vow never to try it again because it was just so fucking delicious and we knew we'd leave the island as crackheads.'

Most of us are never confronted by that situation. Crystal meth and crack aren't physically, psychologically, economically or socially available to us. We are, however, confronted by gingerbread biscuits that seem to gaze pleadingly at us as we order our mid-morning latte. Manufacturers of legal goods have cottoned on to how addiction works and are now repackaging, reformulating and reimagining their products accordingly. As we'll see, manufacturers of packaged food and internet pornography have a meticulously researched grasp of brain science.

The sorts of pleasures people chase vary enormously, from the horny thrill of an MDMA high to the gloopy indulgence of a chocolate sundae. But both these sensations can, in some people, form part of an acceleration of desire – one that requires increasing amounts of exposure in order to maintain levels of pleasure.

Once we realise this, we can see that the old distinction between 'psychological' and 'physical' addiction or dependence is misleading. There are people with eating disorders whose monstrous consumption of ice cream is powerfully reinforced by changes in their brain (which may include a serotonin high if they throw it up). They are physically addicted to it, though this addiction is perfectly reversible if they stop doing this to themselves – and is therefore not a disease in any meaningful sense.

As for the notion of dependence, it can mean many things. Some diabetics are dependent on insulin in the sense that they would die without it. Heroin addicts are dependent on the drug in the sense that they will go into withdrawal without a fix; they won't die from it. A coffee drinker who gets through six espressos a day will also experience withdrawal if he suddenly stops – probably quite a nasty headache; is he therefore not also dependent on caffeine?

In contrast, the terms 'wanting' and 'liking', though they don't sound scientific, can be used unambiguously because they correspond to discrete urges governed by different brain mechanisms. And we can say with some confidence that, increasingly, our wanting urge is overwhelming our liking urge. This is not good news: it tends to bring out the worst in our personalities while overloading our bodies with substances they don't need. Perhaps it's just me, but queuing up for a cappuccino seems like a much less pleasant experience than it was a decade ago: the smell of freshly ground coffee beans seems to sharpen elbows and shorten tempers. But that doesn't matter to vendors whose aim, to put it bluntly, is to make us as greedy as possible.

That was always the case, of course. Presumably even the bakers in ancient Mesopotamia wanted their customers to be greedy. And salesmen have known for centuries that the key to good business lies in the environment – that is, in an artfully arranged backdrop of temptations. Now, however, corporations are learning how to manipulate that environment in order to trigger specific and damaging obsessions. And as we'll see in later chapters, these skills are being developed in every corner of the marketplace. So, if we truly want to understand addiction, we need to examine the disorientating world around us.

4
ENTER THE FIX

The store in the shopping mall has locked its doors. Outside, customers claw helplessly at the windows. Their faces are grey, their eyes dead, their movements jerky and robotic. 'Why do they come here?' one appalled onlooker asks her companion. 'Some kind of instinct, memory – what they used to do,' he replies. 'This was an important place in their lives.'

It was an inspired move of George A. Romero to set his 1978 film *Dawn of the Dead* in the Monroeville Mall, Pennsylvania. The juxtaposition of zombies and a shopping mall captured the public imagination: it seemed such a good fit, somehow. Cinema audiences felt a tweak of recognition as they watched empty-headed people being drawn to the mall like filings to a magnet (especially if they were actually watching *Dawn of the Dead* inside a mall). The zombies criss-crossed the walkways in the aimless patterns of real shoppers, albeit more slowly. Sharp-eyed viewers quickly worked out the director's subversive intentions: *Dawn of the Dead* is a satire on consumer capitalism.

ENTER THE FIX

But do shopping malls actually zombify us? And if so, how? There is a term in pop psychology called the 'Gruen Transfer', named after Victor Gruen, architect of some of America's first malls. The theory goes that some shopping malls are laid out in such a way as to disorientate customers. Exits and routes are obfuscated so that people find themselves led back to stores they left earlier, where a mixture of ambient music, specific lighting and visual cues prompts them to make impulse purchases. According to one account, 'the classic signs that someone is experiencing Gruen Transfer are a dropped jaw, slightly glazed eyes, and a hazy, confused feeling; many people also begin to walk more slowly as this peculiar mental state sets in'.[1]

Compared to the shopping mall of 1978, today's mega-malls offer a near-psychedelic assault on the senses. Westfield Stratford City, a retail centre next to the London Olympic stadium that opened in 2011, contains 300 shops and 70 restaurants on a site the size of 25 football pitches; one bar stocks 50 different champagnes.

There's another Westfield – smaller, but still the size of a dozen cathedrals bolted together – near my home in west London. Last time I visited, plenty of shoppers were displaying the lobotomised expression of the Gruen Transfer. Perhaps this was post-prandial lethargy: a sugar crash after lunchtime feasting on dim sum and Ben & Jerry's.

But other shoppers seemed hyper-vigilant, their eyes darting from side to side, like nervous hunters; one woman looked terrified, as if she was expecting a Marks & Spencer sweater to leap off the counter and strangle her.

What is going on in the minds of these shoppers? You only have to look at them to see that they're surrounded by more choice than their brains can easily handle. Hence the combination of confusion and over-stimulation. They are dazzled by a degree of availability that only the 21st-century retail environment can provide. We've already considered the theory that the more drugs that are available, the more people will run into trouble with them. But shopping malls suggest that the dangers of availability aren't confined to drugs. Put simply, human beings haven't evolved mental defences against the vast range of dangerous temptations they've created in such a short space of time.

In evolutionary terms, we essentially have the brains and bodies of hunter-gatherers. Our biochemistry has changed a bit in response to our dramatically altered surroundings, but not nearly enough for us to be able to adjust to them without damaging ourselves. Most people don't reach the point of becoming addicts; but this mismatch between our bodies and our environment is the fundamental problem of addiction, and it is common to all humanity.

•

Why is shopping for something more fun than owning it? The process of buying that new suede jacket – the window shopping; the decision to try it on; the parading in front of the mirror; the deep breath before we fish out our credit card – leaves a more vivid memory trail than the experience of wearing it. 'Pleasure appears to evaporate when we direct our attention to it,' says the psychiatrist and brain researcher Morten Kringelbach. 'The more we focus on the pleasure itself, the more it slips away.'[2] In contrast, we can easily focus on the events leading to pleasure. To put it another way, it's not the orgasm that lingers in the mind, it's the foreplay.

To make sense of this, we have to keep reminding ourselves that 'wanting' and 'liking' activate different circuits in the brain. Of the two, the dopamine-driven 'wanting' experience is the more powerful and responsive to cues. It's no accident that in everyday conversation we talk more often about seeking pleasure than finding it; looking for a fix than getting it. Sometimes the cue is a reward in itself – not least when we go shopping.

Melinda, a compulsive shopper I met in a 12-step meeting, told me: 'It's all about the thrill in the store. The purchase itself is far more fun than unpacking things when you get home. I barely look at half the shit at the bottom of my wardrobe.'

She's one of those women who like to brag about their shoe and handbag collections to their friends. But secretly she's ashamed about the amount of money she wastes, and she struggles to explain what goes on in her head between picking up the latest season's slingbacks and walking out of the store with them lavishly gift-wrapped. Her ex-husband presumably finds it something of a mystery too.

'I wouldn't call it a black-out, exactly, but something just draws me towards the till. I often find my credit card is already in my hand by the time I get to the front of the queue. I can't wait to jam it in the machine.'

THE FIX

Melinda is no stranger to other sorts of compulsions: she freely admits she drinks too much – punchbowl glasses of Pinot Grigio are an essential component of her Friday night – and she tells me, less enthusiastically, that she used to do a lot of cocaine in her early twenties. But the shopping is what's ruining her life.

Mikey, a self-confessed shopping addict who works in a Manchester bookshop, also has a Pavlovian fixation on watching the plastic work its magic. (Only it's a debit card these days: he's had to cut up all his credit cards to stop him spending money he doesn't have.) 'The biggest kick comes from the little whirr of the card machine when your transaction goes through. It really gets the juices flowing. Honestly, I nearly get a hard-on when I hear it. The most embarrassing thing is that it even works on me when it's someone else's card. Say I'm looking at a sweater, and I hear the machine spitting out a receipt for another customer. At that point, I'm powerless: that sweater is ending up in my wardrobe. After my own receipt is handed over, though, everything is an anticlimax.'

Mikey's reference to sexual arousal isn't that outlandish, from a biological point of view. The anticipation of fulfilment, whether in the form of consumer goods or a sexual encounter, provokes similar neurochemical responses. The juice flowing through Mikey's brain is, of course, dopamine.

Here's where evolutionary theory becomes pertinent. Pleasure isn't an end in itself: the goal of all organisms, not just humans, is to *survive*. Pleasure is a reward for behaviour – conscious or unconscious – that increases our chances of survival. The evolutionary purpose of sex and meals is obvious; but sports, country walks and playing the stock market are also more subtly aimed towards the physical health and material resources that protect us. So you would expect the body to reward people who indulge in them.

In fact, most enjoyable pursuits push us towards desirable evolutionary goals. The problem is, they keep pushing us towards them long after our biological needs have been satisfied. We have no way of switching off the hunter-gatherer instincts inherited from the mammals that preceded us, which have developed over hundreds of thousands of years. Most of the time we're not even aware that they are at work. But, as the evolutionary psychologist Gad Saad argues, they shape even our most trivial consumer preferences.[3]

For example, we like fattening foods because our ancestors needed to store calories in order to ward off starvation. Nearly all human beings, irrespective of their background, prefer juicy burgers to raw broccoli because our taste buds have evolved that way. Women's fashions in most cultures mimic signs of sexual arousal: red lipstick and clothes remind men of the reddening of erogenous zones, while cosmetics generally try to enhance facial symmetry, a genetic indication of good health.

Men buy flashy cars partly as a way of signalling to women their value as a mate: there's more than a kernel of truth in the old joke about penis extensions. But note also that cars, like other status symbols, are objects deployed to bypass long and costly social processes. And the moment of taking possession of the car keys usually provides the new owner with a powerful fix. We're not far removed here from the addict's replacement of people by things.

Social networking websites, meanwhile, cater to our evolved need to connect to others and to draw attention to ourselves. That need is all the stronger because traditional ties of friendship that have glued together societies for thousands of years have been weakened by the very technology that makes Facebook possible. The new networks are fragile in comparison – but, as compensation, they offer a quick route to a fix: an exciting new friendship that stimulates dopamine and can be abandoned when the juice runs out. The 'defriending' and 'blocking' features of social networks are instant replacements for messy interpersonal meltdowns.

Technology and addiction exist in intricate symbiosis. The word 'technology' is shorthand for an infinite number of tools, crafts and techniques that, thanks to scientific discoveries, have the potential to make life more bearable for us – or to tantalise us with the prospect of cheap thrills.

The great rhetorical scholar Kenneth Burke wrote that man is 'separated from his natural condition by instruments of his own making'.[4] Our natural condition is one in which our survival is constantly threatened. Technology keeps those threats at bay, at least for a time, by housing, clothing, feeding and healing us as efficiently as possible. Indeed, the mark of a successful invention is that it allows us to achieve greater rewards for less effort.

ENTER THE FIX

This is a simple point, but worth spelling out. Technology pushes the *work-to-reward ratio* in the direction of rewards – and usually short-term rewards at that. All animals like short-term rewards. That's because, as we've seen, the goal of all organisms is to survive and immediate rewards make that possible. But what other animals can't do – and very few humans could do until recently – is reach out for a quick reward whenever they feel like it.

Unlimited availability can turn a blessing into a curse. Take the example of sugar. We have evolved to like sweet things. Our ancestors recognised fruit as a source of energy. Over countless generations, our internal organs have adjusted to the sort of sugar burst provided by, say, an orange. But what happens when we glug a can of orange soda containing ten times as much sugar as the fruit?

The answer is that our internal organs struggle to cope with this massive ingestion of sugar. But we can't just turn off the brain's ancient urge to gorge on sugar, even though it undermines the health of the rest of our body. The result? A biological-environmental mismatch that has created an epidemic of Type 2 diabetes, a disease which now affects over 300 million people worldwide.[5]

In short, changes in the work-to-reward ratio damage individuals while bringing benefits to society. Sometimes, though, it's difficult to know where the benefits end and the damage begins. Either way, there is an economic incentive for manufacturers and retailers to keep pushing the ratio towards reward. That's what 'economy' means, after all.

As rewards spread throughout society, so does biological maladaptation to our surroundings. In the ancient world, everyone benefited from the inventions of the wheel and the plough. Only privileged individuals, however, could amuse themselves with the fruit of others' labours and fill their stomachs to the point of sickness.

That changed with urbanisation, which did more than satisfy the biological minimum in terms of shelter, clothing and food. Gradually more and more people could indulge themselves, either to the point of satiety – feeling stuffed after a heavy meal – or to the point where they felt a craving for repeated rewards. The towns and cities of the industrial revolution divided labour in a way that forced the poor to work punishingly long hours. But the overall effect of industrialisation was to increase the profitability and availability of short-term rewards. Even factory workers, living on top of each other in conditions of squalor, had access to quick ways of changing their moods.

Capitalism introduced cheap, strong and unhealthy fixes into the lives of all but the poorest citizens of western countries. As an illustration of that process, let's consider the history of the world's most popular psychoactive drug: alcohol.

●

It's possible to become an alcoholic without developing a taste for spirits. I should know. Red wine was my drug of choice, closely followed by beer. Not that I turned my nose up at an offer of whisky, gin or vodka; but I didn't think of spirits as enjoyable drinks so much as a quick route to intoxication. Too quick, really – unless it was a post-pub drinking session, by which time any instinct for self-preservation had long since disappeared.

Spirits can be blamed for proper mass drunkenness, which doesn't seem to have existed before distillation came along. It's true that the Dionysian revellers of ancient Greece drank themselves into a stupor, but only in the limited context of their quasi-religious rituals. No doubt some peasants 3,000 years ago were too fond of wine or beer and earned a reputation as village drunks, but alcoholic drinks weren't regarded as a problem for society as a whole until more recently.

By the twelfth century, monks had learned how to distil grape alcohol, but it was used mainly for medical purposes, as was edible opium in China at the same time. It wasn't until the invention of techniques for distilling cereal crops that the industrial production of very powerful beverages became possible.

Spirits took the relatively mild effects of wine and beer – which helped people to conquer anxiety, strengthen communal bonds and find sexual partners – and refined them into a hit. Their high concentration of ethanol produced faster changes to brain chemistry than any previous beverage. The result was a quicker fix and a greater risk of physical dependence.

That was good news for the people who made and distributed the stuff. It's not just consumers who get more bang for their buck when the work-to-reward ratio of a drug changes like this: so do manufacturers, especially if an addictive spiral is created in which the stronger the commodity, the more insistently customers return for more.

The first recorded epidemic of drunkenness in history – the Gin Craze that hit London in the eighteenth century – followed a dramatic upheaval in the marketplace. In 1690 Parliament blocked imports of French brandy with an Act 'for the encouraging of the Distilling of Brandy and Spirits from Corn'. The monopoly of the London Guild of Distillers was broken; in 1713 Parliament passed another Act allowing anyone to distil spirits without fear of prosecution.

This deregulation had some ugly consequences. Even rotten corn could be turned into gin, producing potent but foul-tasting liquor. As Jessica Warner writes in *Craze*, her study of the epidemic, 'aside from its name, this beverage bore little resemblance to what now passes for gin. It was made from the worst possible ingredients, and because of this it was flavoured with fruits and other additives in an attempt to mask its harsh and musty taste.' Gin was 'the punch of the poor'. The taxes it raised financed the building of an empire while lining the pockets of landowners and the merchant classes.[6]

This morality tale was played out against a background of rapid, disorientating urbanisation. England's capital city was expanding too fast for its own good. To quote the historian Elise Skinner, 'gin sellers thrived in the sprawling suburbs of London because the local authorities were either too weak, corrupt or simply overwhelmed by the number of problems to deal with to adequately respond to the increased consumption. This situation was exacerbated by the absence of magistrates willing or qualified to police these neighbourhoods. Consequently, thousands of women and men were able to sell gin openly and without a licence.'[7]

Many of the gin drinkers were women. The old ale houses were all-male environments, but in the unruly new gin shops of London women were allowed to drink alongside men. This horrified social reformers, who depicted these women as drunken prostitutes who spread syphilis and abandoned their children. The gin-sodden harridan became the focus of respectable anxiety about the craze, rather as vomiting 'ladettes' dominated media depictions of binge drinking in late 1990s Britain.

I've already mentioned Hogarth's engraving *Gin Lane*, set in the London district of St Giles. No one who has seen it can forget the hideous sight of a woman casually dropping her baby to its death. She is half naked, allowing us to see the sores from the syphilis that she has picked up as a prostitute. In the background, another mother tips gin down her infant's throat. A lunatic dances in the street bearing a dead baby impaled on a spike. Drunks fight and stagger outside the busy distiller's shop, which bears the apt name of Kilman. Also thriving is Mr Gripe the pawnbroker, to whom the gin-addicted carpenter is offering his saw and the housewife her cooking utensils. In contrast, the barber is ruined because nobody can afford a haircut or shave. His body dangles from a rope in the attic of his shop.

Gin Lane exaggerated the crisis, as cartoons do, but not by much. One in four houses in St Giles sold gin, which cost only one and a half pennies per cup. Hawkers toured the streets with wheelbarrows of gin, some of it poisonous. In total, five million gallons of spirit were being distilled in London every year. Most gin drinkers got through two pints of it a week.

By the time Hogarth's cartoon appeared in 1751, Parliament was finally ready to take drastic action. In that year, it passed a Gin Act that banned distillers from selling to unlicensed merchants. This, coupled with a rise in grain prices, began to put smaller gin shops out of business. The craze petered out.

Were the gin-sodden victims of the craze 'proper' alcoholics? That's like asking whether the heroin-smoking soldiers in Vietnam were proper addicts. The 12-step fellowships would probably say no, but their understanding of addiction isn't sufficiently flexible to encompass addicted people who return to normal. For a time, the Georgian drinkers were trapped by a dopamine-fuelled desire for repeated doses of a highly refined drug. They consumed it addictively. Then, thanks to circumstances beyond their control, the supply of their drug dried up, as it did for the Vietnam GIs flown home. The amount of gin being produced halved in the decade after the Gin Act. Many people simply abandoned the suicidal drinking habits of the craze.

Common sense tells us that some eighteenth-century gin drinkers were more prone to alcoholism than others, but we don't have the data. Nor do we know much about Vietnam soldiers' individual susceptibility to addiction.

ENTER THE FIX

Such is the paucity of information available to us about addictive epidemics that it is not possible to establish causation with certainty – but in both cases we can trace a correlation between addictive behaviour and availability, the factor so often overlooked in studies of addiction.

To repeat Michael Gossop's argument, people are most likely to run into trouble with a drug if it is economically, socially and psychologically available to them. If all these boxes are ticked, then the scene is set for an epidemic of addiction among people who would not otherwise become addicts. If Parliament had voted differently in 1692, the terrifying crone dropping her baby down the stairwell might have been a happy housewife and a loving mother.

●

Anyone who has read Malcolm Gladwell's *The Tipping Point* will remember how the book opens, with a description of how Hush Puppies went almost overnight from being horribly drab footwear to must-have hipster accessory. Later chapters offer an anatomy of word-of-mouth ecosystems, in which tiny tweaks to the environment can produce dramatic changes in popular behaviour.

Addictive behaviour is fuelled in the same way. The most stupidly self-destructive habits, such as round-the-clock drinking or eating a 3,000-calorie fried chicken breakfast, are typically the product of social epidemics. They are 'sticky', to use Gladwell's terminology. As Nicholas Christakis and James Fowler say in their book *Connected*, never underestimate the tendency of human beings to influence and copy one another. 'Students with studious roommates become more studious. Diners sitting next to heavy eaters eat more food. Homeowners with neighbours who garden wind up with manicured lawns.'[8]

There's a chilling passage in *The Tipping Point* in which Gladwell relates how a horrible example of 'sticky' behaviour, suicide, began spreading among teenage boys in the Micronesian islands. The boys who killed themselves were not obvious candidates for suicide, unlike Hogarth's bankrupt barber. But, somehow, ending their own lives had become an appropriate response to minor setbacks for these young men.

Gladwell says that when we interpret other people's behaviour, we invariably overestimate the importance of character traits and underestimate the importance of situation and context.[9] He's right – and epidemics of addictive behaviour support his argument.

Such epidemics were rare in the past because only occasionally was an addictive substance comprehensively available. But when they did strike, they weren't confined to eccentrics, vagabonds or individuals who were already going off the rails. In the cases of the Gin Craze and the Vietnam heroin epidemic, it was precisely the ordinariness of the addicts that scared the authorities. They couldn't tell who would succumb because everybody was at risk in such a dangerous environment. In Georgian London, it no doubt reawakened dreadful folk memories of the plague.

In the back streets of St Giles and the US barracks in South Vietnam, people found themselves herded together in the middle of an unregulated market in mind-bending intoxicants. Gin and heroin weren't new substances, but in both cases there had been a leap forward in production techniques. In eighteenth-century London there weren't enough magistrates to punish drunks; in Vietnam, the US authorities – who had managed to stamp out marijuana smoking – couldn't detect odourless heroin-laced cigarettes. Also, both populations were disorientated by change. London was expanding at a bewildering pace; the GIs had been transplanted to a battlefield on the other side of the world.

These environmental changes produced a particular variety of social epidemic, the sort that saturates a high-density population. Even people who didn't resort to drugs – and there are *always* people for whom intoxication has no appeal – found their lives altered by them. In the cases we've considered, if just one of the ingredients in the mixture had been different, those epidemics might not have materialised. But we can say that only with hindsight. The one thing we know for certain about social epidemics is that they *can't* be predicted. No one knows exactly which environmental tweaks will lead to sudden change, or what form that change will take.

●

We see a different pattern of social epidemic, for example, in the case of opium smoking in eighteenth-century China – the world's first truly catastrophic drug (as opposed to alcohol) epidemic. The habit spread too slowly to be described as a 'craze' this time, because the supply lines were diffuse, tangled and difficult to eradicate.

THE FIX

The opium epidemic began, as the others had, with a scientific discovery. Europeans picked up the habit of smoking tobacco from American Indians. But it didn't occur to them to smoke opium, even though the drug had been widely used as a mild tranquilliser and aphrodisiac for thousands of years. Smoking it was a Chinese innovation: one that was to prove devastating.

Smoking did for opium what distillation did for alcoholic drinks, because the lungs deliver opium's active ingredients, morphine and codeine, to the brain far more efficiently than the stomach. Users become almost literally high on happiness, since along with dopamine the drug releases the endorphins that soothe emotional pain.

In the nineteenth century Britain notoriously went to war to protect the supply of smuggled opium from British India. The trade was possible only because it was protected by Chinese bureaucrats and warlords who were themselves addicts. This reveals a common feature of addictive epidemics: 150 years later, rogue elements in the Vietnamese government protected the heroin trade, despite the damage it was doing to their country.

Successive Chinese emperors were horrified by the damage done to society. Opium addicts were useless to everyone and prone to persuade other bored people to try smoking the drug. The imperial court tried everything to banish it, including the most barbaric executions of opium dealers in front of Western merchants. But nothing worked. As an edict of 1799 noted, opium smoking had spread from 'vagrants and disreputable people' to 'respectable families, students and officers of the government. When this habit becomes established by frequent repetition, it gains an entire ascendence, and the consumer of opium is not only unable to forbear from its daily use, but on passing the accustomed hour, cannot refrain from tears or command himself in any degree.'

When I read that, I asked an ex-heroin addict friend of mine if it rang true. 'Definitely,' he said. 'Opiate addicts are a lachrymose bunch, emotionally shattered by the thought of going into withdrawal. You see them in the waiting rooms of clinics, comparing notes with desperate self-pity, terrified that they're about to start "clucking".' (That's an in-joke about going cold turkey.)

But, he added, that was more a function of the drug than of their personalities. Websites for relatives trying to wean their loved ones off opiates (usually heroin) are warned to expect tears and tantrums at the mere suggestion of going into treatment. Opiates mimic the endorphin release associated with maternal love: no wonder the prospect of losing the supply induces tears.

However, the Chinese addicts are unlikely to have taken up smoking opium because they desperately needed to experience its soothing euphoria; that came later, when they were dependent on it. There is no point in speculating about their psychological needs – well-documented social factors are far more relevant. It's more likely that they chose opium because it was fashionable, because they were genetically intolerant to alcohol and this was their only available intoxicant, or because they were bored. Opium smoking is a languid, protracted process – it's at the opposite end of the scale from coke-snorting in this respect. It has a special appeal for underemployed rich people, of whom there were an unusual number in imperial China.[10]

The Chinese opium epidemic was shaped by an environmental 'fit' between a particular narcotic and a particular segment of society. You could say the same about the other drug networks we've discussed. The two million Chinese addicts were not concentrated in one place, like the Vietnam GIs and, to a lesser extent, the London gin drinkers. Nonetheless, there is a common denominator: availability.

●

When we think of addiction, the first word that comes to mind is 'drugs'. But perhaps it shouldn't be. According to the sociologist Jacob Avery, our ideas are too heavily influenced by medical research, which concentrates on drugs and their effect on neurotransmitters. He argues that addiction is virtually uncharted territory for sociologists. As a result, not enough attention is paid to 'micro-situations', the small dilemmas of everyday life that ultimately lead people to take what are objectively very bad decisions, but provide them with a comforting emotional pay-off.[11]

Drugs need not come into the picture at all. Let's consider two places that are specifically designed to arouse addictive urges – casinos and strip clubs. They both serve alcohol, but only as an accompaniment to the rituals that lead customers into costly but not substance-based self-indulgence.

ENTER THE FIX

The rites of the blackjack table, for example, are as meticulous as any religious rubric. Like a Catholic priest celebrating an elaborate Latin Mass, the dealer is following a far more detailed script than most members of his congregation realise. The laying out of the wagered bills, the stacking, the dealing of cards, the particular variety of shuffle, the rotation of dealers – all these are intended not just to guarantee the security of the game but also, with their hypnotic formality, to create a state of mind that channels the players' compulsive urges.[12]

Likewise, strip clubs cynically exploit the sexual desire of middle-aged men with calculated theatrical spectacles. You see it so often on screen: a beautiful young woman making exaggerated flirting gestures as she loosens the tie of a sweaty businessman. In the strip club, for a few expensive moments, a man is at the centre of the sexual universe – and, as Avery points out, it's all on display for other males to see. The scene is a grotesque parody of a mating ritual with roots so deep that they stretch across the animal kingdom. Yet the basic rule of strip clubs is that actual mating is forbidden: when the man's hand reaches up, it is slapped down. He may even be thrown out.

Casinos and strip clubs crank up their customers' 'wanting' instincts to a sadistic degree and keep them there. The thrill-seeker is endlessly teased with cues that signify sudden wealth or a glorious sexual encounter. Deep down, he knows that these cues are deliberately misleading – but such is the short-term buzz of excitement that he's prepared to ignore the long-term consequences.

The owners of casinos and strip clubs endlessly tweak their products in order to make them as addictive as possible – but there's no clear dividing line between customers with a 'problem' and recreational visitors. No one is really sure where the dividing line is, including the government, the casinos, the dealers and the patrons themselves.

No explanation of why people succumb to self-destructive temptations is going to be a tidy one. Although social context is important, that context may be too complicated to allow us to place people on a spectrum of addictive behaviour.

What we can do, however, is keep stepping back to remind ourselves of the big picture. The only things limiting our ability to stimulate ourselves to the point of frenzy are our fragile biology and our common sense. Western society has moved beyond the point where addictive epidemics can easily be distinguished from everyday behaviour; the dynamics of addiction and the dynamics of the free market simply have too much in common.

The modern marketplace depends for its smooth functioning on a supply of novel goods that automatically refreshes itself. Dopamine is excited by novelty; so are social networks. It's hard for us, as consumers, to know whether we are paying too much attention to the lovely things dangled in front of us – and whether our desire for them is provoked by peer pressure or brain chemistry. But we usually end up buying them anyway.

●

ENTER THE FIX

'My catarrh has disappeared!' declares a chubby little schoolboy, holding up a long, thin bottle of medicinal syrup. He looks happy. Perhaps he's high. He has, after all, been taking heroin.

The boy appears in an advertisement that ran in a Spanish newspaper in 1912; it's for the heroin syrup that Bayer, a German pharmaceutical company, made for coughs, colds and 'irritation'. In another ad, an elegantly dressed housewife is shown lovingly spooning heroin into her little girl's mouth. *La tos desaparece*, it says – 'the cough disappears'. The campaign had been completely forgotten until critics of Big Pharma dug it up and posted it online in 2011. Most of the ads were targeted at children, but one of them shows the same housewife feeding syrup to her bronchial husband, who has come home wrapped in a heavy scarf. Someone has added the line: 'Hi, honey, here's your smack!'[13]

I'm pretty sure Bayer would have preferred these advertisements to remain forgotten. If you enter the word 'heroin' into the search box on the multinational corporation's website, you will find three brief references to the dangers of heroin abuse but no reference to the fact that Bayer invented the drug diamorphine in 1898 and trademarked it as Heroin, to indicate its 'heroic' properties.

Bayer had been looking for a less addictive alternative to morphine, which had become dangerously popular even in the most respectable circles. In his cultural history of intoxication, *Out of It*, Stuart Walton describes the late Victorian fad for morphine tea parties: 'A society hostess would invite acquaintances around for tea at 4 p.m., after the service of which the ladies would be invited to draw up their sleeves and receive an adorably divine injection from their hostess who – one may assume – was scrupulous to a nicety in observing the hygienic imperatives demanded by needle-sharing.' (One can't help pitying the poor servants, since the side-effects of morphine include dizziness, light-headedness and vomiting.) Some women, Walton reports, even had customised syringes made so they could shoot themselves up during intervals at the ballet.[14]

You might ask what on earth was Bayer thinking – manufacturing a more refined version of morphine and imagining that it would be less addictive than the original? Certainly, within a couple of years of its introduction, the medical community knew that heroin was habit-forming. But, even now, it's not clear that it really is more addictive than morphine. It is faster-acting, because it crosses the blood-brain barrier more quickly. Because of its strength, it costs less to inject. The high is basically the same, though, and far less intense for a first-time user than that produced by, say, crack cocaine.

What turned heroin into an infamous 'demon drug' is that it became readily available on the streets. It didn't occur to anyone that the magic ingredient in a cough syrup would end up being injected by inner-city junkies – but perhaps it should have. History suggests that anyone who develops a powerful psychoactive substance, whether for medical or recreational purposes, is likely to create large-scale addiction – or, to put it another way, a hugely profitable surge in demand.

It's not easy for manufacturers to know how to respond in those circumstances. People like the experience of an instant and painless chemical reward – and I'm using the word 'reward' loosely here, to include marvellously effective painkillers. Even when that reward ceases to be painless and they no longer get much pleasure out of the substance, the 'wanting' persists: as Gene Heyman emphasises, the non-reasoning parts of our brains don't distinguish between the use and abuse of drugs. They don't distinguish between legal and illegal drugs, either – or cheap and expensive ones.

This is where biology and supply-and-demand economics collide. The 'wanting' urge is so strong that demand for illegal drugs is inelastic, which means that, when police seize enough quantities of a drug to increase its street price – usually only temporarily – the market for it doesn't shrink proportionately. People value their fix so much that they go to extra efforts to obtain it. Although decreased supplies provoke turf wars among drug dealers, addicts still clamour for their wares.[15]

If the supply of a drug could be permanently restricted and there were no alternatives, then demand for it would fall, albeit slowly. But these days there are always alternatives, even for the most desperate addicts. Health professionals who work in highly addicted communities report that if there is a sudden shortage of a particular drug in a city, users will switch to something else – from heroin to cocaine, for example, even though the effect of these two drugs on the brain is very different.

Also, it's becoming clearer to scientists that non-substance addictions can perform many of the same functions, and do much of the same damage, as drugs or alcohol. We touched briefly on the puzzle of comorbidity in the previous chapter. People who give up a mind-altering drug often develop obsessive relationships with other things. Ex-drunks will start binge eating, for example. I remember being at an AA meeting at which a borderline obese Catholic priest announced: 'I gave up the bottle only to fall headfirst into a tub of Häagen-Dazs.'

The notion that human beings have addictive urges which can be transferred from one object or substance to another has incredibly far-reaching implications. Science has a long way to go before it pieces together the jigsaw. But it only takes a visit to a major retail centre to realise that brands and businesses are learning more and more about our addictive vulnerabilities – and how to exploit them. And can we really blame them? It's called making a profit.

Addictive behaviours aren't necessarily locked on to specific things: in a world where there are practically limitless pleasurable experiences on offer, obsessive behaviour becomes promiscuous: it can grab hold of any object or activity that promises us a hit.

●

These days, I still spend up to £100 a week on my own fix. I visit my dealer whenever I can, desperately hoping that he has something that will make my dopamine levels jump. Such as, for example, a recording of the little-known Russian pianist Dmitri Bashkirov playing a Schubert piano sonata.

ENTER THE FIX

I know how pretentious this sounds, but I'm addicted to buying CDs of classical music. I'm not addicted to listening to them. I do listen to lots of classical music, and derive intense pleasure from it, but I'm quite capable of buying a CD and leaving it for weeks in its shrink-wrap. You see, it's already done its job: it was the experience of finding it that excited my dopamine pathway.

There are more than 3,000 classical CDs on my shelves. Many of them contain pieces of music that move and fascinate me so intensely that I've spent decades thinking about them and comparing recordings. Beethoven's *Hammerklavier* Sonata, for example. I have 25 versions and even that's not enough: every reading brings me closer to grasping the mysterious symmetry of its slow movement, or the crazed mathematics of the final fugue.

I don't listen to it as a fix. But I *buy* CDs of it as a fix, along with innumerable discs of music that mean far less to me and that I want in my collection because I'm what critics refer to as a 'completist'. This is the obsessive-compulsive side of addiction, as yet little understood by scientists. Connoisseurs of internet pornography collect thousands of images because it gives them a similar kick, as we'll see later. Thankfully, I've settled on something more harmless.

My obsession is supply-driven by digital technology: I couldn't have done the same thing when there were only five available recordings of the *Hammerklavier*, which was the case in the 1960s. To look at it another way, digitalisation has had the same explosive effect on the supply of classical recordings as it has on the supply of porn.

I thought this particular addiction of mine was unusual, until my oldest schoolfriend told me that, during the collapse of his first marriage, he was buying hundreds of CDs of classical music, many of which he still hadn't unwrapped. 'To be honest, I think it was one of the reasons we split up,' he added.

Then I read a book called *In the Realm of Hungry Ghosts* by Dr Gabor Maté, a physician who treats homeless addicts in downtown Vancouver. It's full of extraordinary insights into the lives of people tortured by every form of substance abuse and violence. But, for me, by far the most memorable passage is the one in which Maté – who has never struggled with substance addictions – describes his particular problem.

'Hello, my name is Gabor, and I'm a compulsive classical music shopper,' he says.

When things were at their worst, Maté was visiting Sikora's, the classical music store in Vancouver, several times a week. He would spend more than a thousand dollars a month on his splurges. And when he wasn't in Sikora's, he was at home poring over online music reviews, something I do myself for hours at a time.

'As soon as the reviewer says something like "no self-respecting lover of symphonic/choral/piano music should be without this set", I'm done for,' he writes.[16] Suddenly he cannot imagine life without this new set of period-instrument Haydn symphonies, or his third version of Mozart's complete violin concertos or yet another 14-CD cycle – his fifth – of Wagner's *Ring* cycle.

ENTER THE FIX

I've just counted my own Wagner cycles: Bodansky/Leinsdorf, Keilberth, Solti, Böhm, Goodall, plus Levine and Boulez on DVD and Furtwängler's incomplete set. Of these, my favourite is probably the Keilberth, because it's the one the critics have praised most extravagantly (when I'm outside my area of musical speciality, I have a lazy habit of allowing critics to dictate my judgements) and, shamingly, *because it has the nicest packaging.*

CD boxes are not things of beauty, as some LPs were, but the neatness and smartness of the package influences the way I think about the music. It's why I can't get excited about downloading – though, like a true obsessive, I organise my iTunes library fastidiously. Yesterday I went hunting for a CD that I can download much more cheaply from the eMusic website. When I didn't find it, my joyful anticipation seeped away and I could restore my spirits only by buying *five* discs of music that I didn't want nearly as much. Which reminds me: I must play them some time.

Visitors to my flat look in amazement at the thousands of CDs in purpose-built bookcases and say they admire my absorption in the world of music. They'd be surprised if they knew how few concerts I can be bothered to drag myself to. What they're really looking at is a middle-aged man who has found a socially respectable way of replacing people by things. In slightly different circumstances, it could have been stamps. But thank God it wasn't.

5

WHY CAKE IS
THE NEW COKE

It is time to look at some examples of addictive behaviour in a bit more detail. Let's start with something that is part of everyone's life. Of all the patterns of behaviour that pull us in the direction of compulsion and threaten to take over our lives, none is more pervasive than our new attitude towards food.

Were there always so many fat people at Victoria Station? Most evenings, as I leave my office in the *Daily Telegraph* and walk across the concourse, I can hear young commuters panting like elderly spaniels after rushing to catch their train. Many of them are clutching over-filled baguettes that are impossible to eat without smearing yourself in mayonnaise; they have to lick it off their fingers before fishing for their tickets.

Across the station concourse, a gigantic free-standing food counter groans under the weight of thousands of pieces of loose candy: jelly beans, toffees, bonbons, liquorice sticks, fudge and lollipops, all glistening with artificial colouring. The customers look awfully furtive as they scoop candy into the paper bag before it's weighed. Anyone would think they were picking up pornographic magazines, from the way their shoulders hunch and their eyes dart sideways.

Between 1993 and 2009 the percentage of overweight men in England rose from 59 to 68 per cent; the number of overweight women from 51 to 59 per cent.[1] The trend isn't hard to spot at Victoria, where people from every background rub shoulders.

Inside the *Telegraph* office, however, it's a different story. In this predominantly middle-class environment, any extra pounds are offset by competitive dieting among the feature writers and fashion journalists. What I have noticed, however, is the ever-increasing intrusion of food into the working day, and especially the little afternoon food rituals surrounding 'treats', as we call them. The appearance of treats produces gurgles of childish delight from the most hard-bitten reporters – unsurprisingly, since this is children's party food.

The archetypal treat is called a mini-bite, and it's an invention of the devil. Mini-bites take the most indulgent cakes and desserts and distil them into morsels: chocolate cake, millionaire's shortbread, raspberry doughnuts – all shrunk to a size that absolves you of guilt. If you only eat one, that is. Unfortunately, they're sold in buckets large enough to be visible from five desks away.

And so the ritual begins. What I'm about to describe happens in the comment section of the *Daily Telegraph* in London, but I'm sure that it's replicated, with only minor variations, in offices across Britain and America.

'Ooh!' Somebody has spotted a colleague approaching the desk with two tubs of mini-bites – different varieties, of course. The 'ooh!' is shrill with suppressed excitement; everyone looks up. The tubs are deposited on the desk. There's a moment of silence as the urge for instant gratification does battle with fear of being the first person to crack.

Then one employee – often the head of department – walks up to the tubs and surveys them quizzically, as if this whole 'mini-bite' concept is new to him. He opens the lid gingerly, extracts a treat, inserts it into his mouth … and within seconds the gang descends. Some people manage a perfunctory 'I really shouldn't' before diving in. They tend to be the ones who pay the most return visits to the tubs.

Those journeys from desk to mini-bites and back again are fun to watch. It's hard to do anything surreptitiously in an open-plan office, but people try their best, assuming an expression of studied absent-mindedness as they reach out for one last chocolate cornflake cluster on their way back from an unnecessary trip to the photocopier. (I speak from experience.)

What we're seeing is the battle between the Stop and Go mechanisms in the brain turned into office pantomime. Such is the power of sugar.

●

Most middle-class people have their own mental image of the 'obesity crisis' in Britain and America. It involves blue-collar workers and ethnic minorities who spend every spare minute stuffing themselves with cheeseburgers.

Hollywood documentaries and bestselling books encourage us to think this way – though they are careful not to attack low-paid fat people for their weakness in giving in to temptation. In 2004, for example, the filmmaker Morgan Spurlock made a compelling but self-righteous documentary entitled *Supersize Me*. He spent 30 days eating nothing but McDonald's meals, by the end of which he had gained 30 pounds and suffered heart palpitations.

His first supersized meal consisted of a Double Quarter Pounder with Cheese, Super Size French fries, and a 42-ounce Coca-Cola. Conveniently for the filmmakers, this made him throw up in the car park. The impression left by the movie was that McDonald's was effectively poisoning lower-income families by addicting them to junk food. Indeed, it ended by addressing McDonald's customers: 'Who do you want to go first, you or them?'

Supersize Me won a Grand Jury award at the Sundance film festival. One can understand why it went down so well. For *bien pensant* audiences, it's comforting to think that food addiction is all about easily identifiable villains (fast-food corporations) and victims (low-paid families who eat at McDonald's because they can't afford healthy food).

Comforting – but how accurate? In 2011 a major US study found that households earning $80,000 were more likely to buy junk food than those earning $30,000. *Atlantic* magazine sounded mortified by this discovery: 'It's not cash-strapped Americans who are devouring the most Big Macs and Whoppers, it's us!'[2]

The study was a useful corrective to all the finger-pointing at working-class people that accompanies the obesity debate. But perhaps we should stop talking so much about burgers, fries and the saturated fat they contain, because there's growing evidence that sugar, not fat, is having the biggest distorting effect on our diets. It's leaving middle-class people in particular with 'food issues', as they're euphemistically known. Hence the cupcake craze.

We know that sugar is bad for us: along with fat and salt, it's one of the unholy trinity of modern food additives. We don't necessarily know *how* bad it is for us, though. Lobbying against saturated fats has been so effective that diet-conscious consumers imagine there's a simple correlation between how much fat you eat and your risk of heart disease. There isn't. Sugar is just as bad for your arteries because it contributes directly to obesity and diabetes, both of which put you at greater risk of a heart attack than simply eating a high-fat diet.

Sugar is a fat-free substance that just happens to be massively fattening. Morgan Spurlock may have eaten his way through 12 pounds of fat when he supersized himself, but the real damage to his waistline and his internal organs was done by the 30 pounds of sugar he ingested. However, since it came from fizzy drinks served but not manufactured by his arch-villains McDonald's, the movie didn't stress the point.

In February 2011, a team of researchers from the University of California, San Francisco, published a report in the journal *Nature* entitled 'Public health: The toxic truth about sugar'.[3] This dismissed the popular notion of sugar as 'empty' calories. On the contrary, they were *bad* calories. 'A little is not a problem, but a lot kills – slowly,' said the authors, who went on to propose that sugary foods should be taxed and their sales to children under 17 controlled.

We have known for years that refined sugar is also implicated in damaging the liver and kidneys and is the main cause of the worldwide spread of Type 2 diabetes. 'If these results were obtained in experiments with any illegal drug, they would certainly be used to justify the most severe form of retribution against those unfortunate enough to be caught in possession of such a dangerous substance,' writes Michael Gossop of the National Addiction Centre at King's College, London.[4]

But is sugar actually a drug? Gossop thinks so. If a casual visitor from another galaxy were to drop in on planet earth, he would assume that human beings were even heavier drug users than we already are. Why? Because vast numbers of us ingest a white crystalline substance several times a day. We become agitated if we run out of supplies, and produce lame excuses for why we need another dose. We say we rely on it for 'energy', but we're deluding ourselves. The energy rush from sugar is followed by a corresponding crash: it's physiologically useless. But it is strongly reminiscent of the ups and downs associated with, say, cocaine.

The idea that sugar has some of the psychoactive qualities of recreational drugs is looking more and more credible. One of the major research findings of the past decade has been that sugar can turn rats into classic addicts. A team of scientists from the psychology department of Princeton University put rats on an intermittent diet of large quantities of sugar solution in addition to their normal food. The diet was intermittent because the researchers wanted to see what would happen when the rats were deprived of sugar. The answer was that they went into withdrawal, quivering with anxiety like a junkie deprived of his fix. And when the sugar reappeared, they binged.[5]

Most interesting of all was the finding that, in one key respect, sugar behaves like cocaine and amphetamine. It was already known that if you get a rat hooked on one of these drugs and break off the supply, a week later it will become hyperactive in response to even a tiny dose of that drug, which has no effect on a rat that has never been given the drugs. The period of addiction has 'sensitised' it to the substance. Indeed, the rats are cross-sensitised: a rat previously hooked on cocaine will respond hyperactively to a tiny dose of amphetamine and vice versa. This squares with what we can observe of human addicts, though for ethical reasons they can't be put through the same tests.

What the Princeton team confirmed was that you can replace amphetamine or cocaine with sugar and the same thing happens. A rat previously hooked on sugar is sensitised to amphetamine/cocaine and vice versa. The conclusion the scientists drew from this is that sugar releases dopamine into the nucleus accumbens in a similar way to these drugs. This evidence, published in 2008, is the closest we have to proof that sugar is genuinely addictive.

WHY CAKE IS THE NEW COKE

The same doesn't seem to be true of fat. We naturally like fatty foods: they're more palatable and we have therefore evolved a preference for them. (In the faintly disgusting terminology of the food industry, fat adds to the slipperiness of the mouthfeel.) But fat isn't psychoactive in the same way that sugar is.

If, however, you combine sugar and fat, as human beings have been doing for thousands of years, then a number of evolutionary impulses converge. All satisfying foods release comforting endorphins in our brains; but in the case of, say, chocolate, the opioid pleasure is reinforced by the dopamine hit of mildly psychoactive sugar, which slips down easily thanks to the smooth fatty texture. Salt and fat make a formidable combination, too, definitely more than the sum of its parts, but it doesn't seem to have the same power to persuade people to eat beyond satiety: you may have a deep love of Kentucky Fried Chicken and get fat as a result, but you're less likely to eat it until you feel sick.

Think back to the last office party you attended, and what was left over afterwards. I wonder if there has *ever* been an office 'do' in which people had to clear away half-eaten boxes of chocolates and tubs of mini-bites – but didn't need to throw away any sandwiches because they'd all been wolfed down. I doubt it. Cake is occasionally unfinished because it's filling. Even then, however, it tends to be saved for later rather than discarded, unlike the poor sandwiches (which, admittedly, don't keep as well as cake). Super-sugary doughnuts, however, never make it to the end of the party.

It would be interesting to know what proportion of sweet as opposed to savoury food ends up in the world's bins. My guess is that, not to put too fine a point on it, sweet items are far more likely to be turned into sewage than garbage. The Princeton experiments on rats explain why this might be. If sugar has a special relationship with the dopamine receptors in our brains, then it has the edge over fat and salt in triggering our 'wanting' impulses.

I asked Henry Dimbleby, who runs the Leon chain of restaurants, whether he thought office workers were becoming more preoccupied with sugar. 'Oh, definitely. Sugar is our number one eating problem – I think 40 per cent of the population has some sort of addiction to it,' he said.

Then, quite unprompted, he came out with an analogy between cake and coke. 'Watch what happens in an office when somebody walks in carrying a box of Krispy Kreme doughnuts. There's a general squealing sound and everyone rushes over excitedly. You'd think someone had just arrived at a party with a few grams of coke. People descend on it in the same way. I suppose that's because the effect it has on you is pretty similar.'

Krispy Kreme wouldn't like that suggestion, of course – but the fortunes of this doughnut company, founded by Vernon Rudolph in Winston-Salem, North Carolina in 1937, are an object lesson in how to market ultra-sugary recreational food in an era preoccupied with healthy eating. Like the Magnolia Bakery's cupcakes, Krispy Kreme doughnuts play the nostalgia card. The spelling of the name is amusingly archaic; the logo has not changed significantly since it was designed by Benny Dinkins, a local architect, in the 1930s. During the 1990s, the chain expanded hugely and eventually over-reached itself. Customers who had persuaded themselves that eating old-fashioned doughnuts was an ironic gesture developed pangs of guilt; hastily opened stores had to be closed.

But then the company played with the formula, developing 'signature coffees' to go with the doughnuts. In November 2011 the *Wall Street Journal* reported that Krispy Kreme's fiscal third-quarter earnings had risen 97 per cent.[6] This is what you might call the Starbucks defence for eating pastries between meals: if it's with coffee, you have permission. Where Starbucks has the edge over Krispy Kreme, however, is that its blueberry muffins can be disguised as breakfast; beginning the day with bright pink doughnuts, in contrast, is hard to carry off without arousing suspicions of 'food issues'.

The habit of eating breakfast muffins – or, for the more refined palate, *pain au chocolat* – has become so familiar in London that it's easy to forget that it was almost unknown in Britain until the early 1990s, when the first American-style coffee shops appeared. One wonders how their customers would react if, suddenly, all the shops closed and they had to revert to tea, cereal and toast. A bit like the rats in the Princeton experiment, perhaps.

Admittedly, muffins for breakfast are not the norm in Britain, yet. But there's nothing random about a shift in taste towards a foodstuff carefully targeted towards the pleasure centres in the brain. Likewise, the afternoon 'treats' that materialise on office desks carry overtones of celebration and reward.

That couldn't be said of the custard creams pushed round by the tea lady in the offices of my parents' generation, welcome though the distraction undoubtedly was. Of course, biscuits were basically just compressed sugar and fat, but in such small quantities that people didn't feel strongly about them. The ritual of the tea trolley, if you can call it that, was an emotionless affair: there was little sign of people struggling with their appetites, trying to reconcile the demands of the lower-order Go impulse and the higher-order instruction to Stop. Custard creams just aren't that exciting.

Food dilemmas of the I-really-shouldn't variety were reserved for the formal settings of afternoon tea and dinners when guests were present. Cake was not taken lightly: it was a home-baked gesture of hospitality or – and I'm thinking of my own childhood here – a reward for trudging around a department store on a Saturday afternoon.

Now it's everywhere. The *Sunday Times* columnist India Knight complains that her local high street doesn't have a single butcher's, 'but we have six cake shops, as if we had been sponsored by Marie Antoinette'.[7]

'It's funny stuff, cake,' says Henry Dimbleby. 'It's a mood-changer. We always bring cake to a difficult meeting – it's amazing how people unbend and become more flexible when there's a great gooey chocolate sponge in front of them. I came back to the office the other day with samples of different cakes for my colleagues to try. It caused so much more excitement than if I'd come back with, say, chicken samples. The responses were quite emotional – "I *adore* carrot cake," one girl told me, as if she were revealing a private relationship.'

●

A private relationship. That's a good choice of words. These days not only do we have more of a 'relationship' with food than previous generations did, but it also has an intimate quality. And this despite the fact that we eat meals in public more often than ever before: it's not remotely uncommon for a young professional working in a big city to eat out three or four nights a week.

These excursions are more social than communal. The setting, company and food change daily. Each occasion is the outcome of multiple choices and negotiations – not something you could say of the family meals of earlier centuries, in which the only choice was exercised by a housewife with narrow and predictable options.

If our grandparents could have seen people in their twenties and thirties meeting for supper in the local brasserie, they would have assumed there was a celebration in progress: diners scanning the menu for their favourite dishes – 'I can never resist the calamari' – to the sound of laughter amplified by alcohol. These are office 'treats' writ large.

When we eat out we aren't simply storing away energy; nor are we reinforcing the same set of family bonds day after day. We choose our dining companions for their entertainment value. And when our eyes land on an item on the menu that we 'can't resist' – well, the phrase gives the game away. From the moment we enter the restaurant, our dopamine receptors are in a state of high alert – far more so than they are at the routine family meals that are slowly being squeezed out of western lifestyles. The aroma of entertainment, choice and reward that lingers over the table stimulates the brain's reward circuits – and that's even before we're confronted by food that is engineered to override the Stop mechanism in our frontal lobes.

We've reached a stage at which nearly all eating in public, whether in smart restaurants or fast-food joints, is more about fix than fuel. The amount of time we spend fussing over menu choices, and our habit of changing our minds right at the last minute, indicates how determined we are to extract just the right degree and quality of pleasure from the meal – even if all we end up ordering is a Zinger Tower Burger.

'There's far more ordering off-menu compared to ten years ago,' says Henry Dimbleby. And it's often a painfully intense business: you would think that the customers were going to be held responsible for their choices at the Last Judgement.

This isn't a simple example of the replacement of people by things, because an amusing selection of friends is crucial to these suppers. But the gathering is transient – and, these days, even young, carefree diners behave like middle-aged foodies. 'It's food porn, really,' says Amy, a writer in her mid-twenties whose friends live in the trendier postcodes of east London. 'We're all heavily into photographing the dishes when they arrive – especially if we're somewhere really fancy and there's this amazingly lush ravioli with shaved truffles in front of us.'

Amy and her well-heeled friends have a complicated, even tormented, relationship with food. They treat haute cuisine with a respect that isn't just a tribute to the chef; it's also flavoured with fear, because they know that it makes them put on weight. It's hard to subscribe to the belief – as the girls certainly do – that 'nothing tastes as good as skinny feels' without feeling mildly uneasy in a restaurant. If they order off-menu, it's usually so that the chef leaves out a calorific ingredient.

These young gourmets often starve themselves before and after a heavy meal, and for some of them the option of 'purging' is always at the back of their minds. Thanks to the media, we're used to thinking of bulimia as an illness whose ravages are comparable to severe anorexia. We hear less about the occasional throwing-up that – as restaurant lavatory cleaners will confirm – accompanies meals where a stressed-out but not routinely bulimic diner has lost control of her (more rarely, his) appetite.

In the words of one cynical observer: 'If I see a woman disappear into the loos in between courses and return with a smile on her face, I think: either she's just barfed and is feeling deliriously happy at having wiped the slate clean, or she's refilled on the nose candy. If the latter, she won't eat a damn thing for the rest of the evening, though she won't hold back on the wine.'

In metropolitan circles, different tribes have their own ways of resolving food issues. Here's a disconcerting one. 'Gay men in London are very keen on the weight loss pills called Alli,' says Dr Max Pemberton, a psychiatrist working in a London hospital. Alli is called Xenical in the United States, where it is prescription-only. Its effects are dramatic: it stops the body absorbing fat and is recommended only for overweight people. Alli can be sold over the counter in Britain, but only by pharmacists, who are supposed to check that the customer really needs it. It's a popular product generally, but especially in the gay community, where putting on weight is regarded as a cardinal sin. 'There are gay-friendly pharmacists who'll hand it over to guys who just want to go out to dinner without putting on weight,' says Pemberton.

'It has one notorious side effect – anal leakage. Let's not go into too much gory detail. But regular users know the score. They take the pill *after* they've eaten their fatty food, which delays the gruesome side effects until later that night.' Which is fine, presumably, so long as you aren't planning to take a date home with you.

Of course, most people don't throw up or cut corners with slimming pills. But growing numbers of us have an unstable relationship with food. We're conscious of its mood-fixing – and mood-destroying – potential. Hence the little dramas in restaurants; hence, too, the distracted and unhappy atmosphere in many supermarkets, especially the upmarket ones that disguise their microwaveable goodies as restaurant courses.

WHY CAKE IS THE NEW COKE

Most evenings after work, I stop off at the Marks & Spencer food hall at Victoria Station. It can be a nightmare to fight your way through to the tills – not just because the store is crowded, but because of the way customers hover in the aisles, slack-jawed with indecision while their gaze wanders from the Cajun Chicken Fettuccine to the Salmon en Croûte and back again. Frequently people stand balancing a pre-packaged meal in each hand, wondering which of them will yield more pleasure or guilt when the microwave oven pings. And that's before they get on to the *really* serious business of choosing a pudding.

That's where the manufacturer's statistics come in handy. Middle-class shoppers are painfully aware of the trade-off that comes with indulgent food. Your body pays a price; the numbers on the back of the packet help you decide whether it's worth it. Actually, given that shoppers tend to fixate on the calorie and fat totals but gloss over the sugar content, it may not be a well-informed decision. Nevertheless, the calculations increase their identification with the food – the 'personal relationship' created by the fusion of compulsion and choice.

Marks & Spencer likes to give the impression that it helps shoppers avoid clogging up their arteries by accident. 'We all know we should follow a healthy diet, but it's not always obvious what's good for you and what isn't. So we've worked it out for you,' it declares patronisingly.[8] That's true, in the sense that its food carries 'nutritional information' and, like all supermarkets, it offers low-fat versions of dishes. They're not low-reward options, though; if anything, they seek to be even more enticing.

Henry Dimbleby insists that cutting out the fat doesn't do anything for customers' health: 'When supermarkets take the fat out of their lasagne, they probably replace it with highly refined starch which gives it a smoother, luxurious feel but has a high glycaemic index. Plus, they may throw in lots of sugar. This 'low-fat' thing could really be a con. You'd be much better off with the original version.'

The Marks & Spencer food hall meticulously exploits the middle-class determination to turn even the most routine home dining experiences into an imitation of a luxury dinner party – or a children's birthday bash. There are iced cakes everywhere. But M&S isn't unique in this respect.

In the summer of 2011, I visited what may be the world's yuppiest supermarket: Whole Foods in Palo Alto, California, which believes in 'promoting the health of our stakeholders [customers] through healthy eating education'. When I arrived, 'stakeholders' were busy trying free samples of the fattest cupcakes I've ever seen. ('They're so big, it's hard to get a full bite,' complained one online reviewer.) According to Whole Foods, each vanilla cupcake has 480 calories, which I would have thought was a conservative estimate.

The customers crowding around the display wore Birkenstock sandals and T-shirts with radical slogans. They were also enormous. A conservative Californian friend of mine has coined the term 'activist butt' to describe the huge posteriors of middle-aged women protesting about American foreign policy, welfare cuts or whatever. Clearly, despite what you might read in the liberal British press, there isn't a precise correlation between obesity and voting Republican.

Whole Foods says it's 'passionate' about the sourcing and ingredients of its products. References to 'passion' are easily the most cringeworthy corporate cliché of recent decades, but the threads on the Whole Foods blog suggest that lots of its customers *are* passionate about these things. Would they feel so strongly if they hadn't built up an unusually strong 'personal relationship' with food? No. What makes that relationship so strong isn't only the company's ethical sourcing or commitment to healthy eating. It's the addictive deliciousness of its products, whose price tags suggest that the liberal management knows exactly how to cash in on bourgeois food anxieties.

Imagine if Whole Foods really did make the health of its stakeholders its priority. The in-your-face display of cupcakes would have to go, because however responsibly harvested their ingredients are, and however magically free of trans fats they may be, those cakes are *junk food*. Likewise, if Marks & Spencer was serious about telling its customers what is and isn't good for them, it would have to slap diabetes warnings on dozens of 'indulgent' puddings and cakes, and probably its low-fat savoury dishes as well.

But then, of course, it would go out of business. So would any supermarket, grocer's, bakery or restaurant that failed to satisfy the increasingly detailed demands of the 21st-century customer. These are framed differently depending on people's background and beliefs:

some focus on value for money, some on the quality of the food, some on its perceived healthiness, some on the ethical purity of the sourcing. But at the heart of all these demands lie ever-rising expectations of self-gratification. And the higher those expectations become, the closer we move towards addiction.

●

How do you tell the difference between a normal drinker and an alcoholic? The normal drinker says: 'I'm going to the pub tonight and I'll get totally smashed.' The alcoholic says: 'I'm going to the pub tonight and I *won't* get totally smashed.'

I can't remember at which AA meeting I heard that saying, but never has a truer word been spoken. It wasn't the amount I drank that persuaded me I was an alcoholic; it was my pathetic inability to predict when I would get plastered. Sometimes I could surprise myself by walking away from a boozy dinner having drunk only a couple of glasses. More often, an innocuous 'quick pint' after work would turn into *The Lost Weekend*. Either way, the challenge of managing my alcohol intake absorbed an awful lot of mental energy.

A whole generation of problem eaters are discovering the same thing about food. Resisting temptation is almost a full-time job for people who, when they walk through a shopping centre, find a different 'wanting' urge stimulated every time they turn their head.

The 12-step fellowships have an acronym for these situations. HALT: Hungry, Angry, Lonely, Tired. If you're experiencing any combination of those feelings, you're more likely to reach for a sweet, fatty or salty fix. This is no secret to purveyors of fast food – they do good business in places where people feel hassled and isolated. Look at Victoria Station.

Usually it's not hard to tell who regularly gives in to temptation. One woman I know claims to be able to spot a bulimic at ten paces: 'They never learn that there's no such thing as a perfume that covers up the whiff of you-know-what. Also, yellow teeth on a pretty girl are a dead giveaway – it's the stomach acid.'

Ultimately, though, there's no infallible way of spotting someone with food 'issues', because some of the most troubled people never act on their fears and fantasies.

In his book *The End of Overeating*, Dr David Kessler, former commissioner of the US Food and Drug Administration, interviewed his colleagues about their favourite snacks – the treats that made their mouths water. He found that thin people as well as fat ones had developed powerful, intimate and angst-ridden obsessions with cookies and chocolate. They weren't secretly purging; they had strategies for managing these distractions.

A thin woman called Rosalita talked about the way she always left food on her plate in order to compensate for her M&M binges. But her management technique would fall to pieces if a co-worker brought cookies into the office. 'I'll eat one, go to my desk, then think about them. Then I'll go back for another one. And I'll do that for the rest of the afternoon.'[9]

Why doesn't Rosalita stop herself getting up from her desk for another cookie? It would be wrong to say that she's compelled to scarf another biscuit by her brain chemistry. She is not a typical addict, but she does have a very impulsive and unhealthy relationship with food.

The tricky concept of food addiction forces us to confront the growing grey area between normal behaviour and fully fledged addictions that ruin people's lives. As we've seen, sugar induces cocaine-like reactions in mice. Other foodstuffs don't, but we have an evolutionary preference for fat and salt, so we eat them in unhealthy quantities even if we don't experience the same dopamine cascade that we do with sugar.

'Food' is shorthand for any number of substances, some more drug-like than others in their ability to change our moods. So when the media talk about 'food addiction', or even 'junk food addiction', it's not quite clear what sufferers are supposed to be addicted *to*. You couldn't say that of alcohol or heroin. Also, obviously we all have to eat – most of us in an environment saturated with temptations.

These ambiguities create confusion, but they're also revealing. Food addictions – and the addictive behaviour inspired by food – are more deeply embedded in the daily routines of society than any other form of over-consumption. The need to search for food drove the evolution of our brains; it moulded the first communities; it has left its traces on our most sacred rituals. So when this instinct is mercilessly tweaked by addictive impulses, no wonder it unsettles us.

David Kavanagh, a professor of clinical psychology at the University of Queensland, captures the unique misery caused by an obsession with tasty food: it's a sort of guilty longing. As he tells Kessler, 'there's a lot of parallel stuff that's occurring when people are trying to engage in control at the same time they are experiencing a desire'.[10] Different factions in the brain are slugging it out again – but in this case the outcome is usually predictable, since food desire is so much stronger than food control.

'Conditioned hypereating' is Kessler's term for our greedy but often angst-ridden consumption of unhealthy food. He uses the word 'conditioned' because the food industry not only engineers food that exploits our natural preference for sugar, fat and salt, but also grabs our attention when we're not eating, employing cues that awaken our wanting instinct.

We've already seen that the dopamine receptors in our brains naturally fasten on to cues. The sight of an actor in a black-and-white Hollywood film insouciantly lighting up a cigarette can be enough to reactivate nicotine craving in someone who hasn't smoked in years.

Food cues can also be switched on at any time of day; ingenious manufacturers can make people desire food at a time when they're normally doing something else. The gold medal in this field has to go to Starbucks and its Frappuccino. The word is a portmanteau of the French *frappé*, meaning chilled (or, in the case of coffee, shaken) and cappuccino. It was invented by a Massachusetts coffee chain which sold the rights to it when it was bought by Starbucks.

Suddenly Starbucks had an answer to a problem that had been dogging it for years. During the afternoon, its usually busy stores were 'so empty that you could roll a bowling ball through them', according to a venture capitalist interviewed by Kessler.[11] But this rich, sweet milkshake pick-me-up was perfect for that 4 p.m. lull.

This I know from experience, because I used to work in the big tower at Canary Wharf, where Starbucks had installed a store just at the bottom of the lifts. Every afternoon during the summer I would descend 12 storeys to slurp a Frappuccino, always hoping that the barista would keep the ice in the shaker long enough for it to be properly ground – and also would remember that the caramel drizzle came free with the whipped cream. I hated the embarrassment of having to put him right on that point.

I stopped because I was getting fat. Those 'empty' calories were giving me one hell of a paunch – and, I now learn from *Nature* magazine, further increasing my risk of an early death. But there's no getting away from it: those mocha Frappuccinos hit the spot.

The research into overeating is actually quite frightening. The vulnerabilities it exposes are almost universal, and the trends in society – despite all the lavishly funded campaigning for healthy eating – are still moving steadily in the direction of hypereating.

Our new eating habits – and in terms of the history of *Homo sapiens* they are very new indeed – represent a profound mismatch of our appetites and our biological needs. High-calorie foods that once represented a precious opportunity to store energy now attack the internal organs of our sedentary bodies.

●

The problem is even worse than we might imagine, however, because researchers have uncovered two nasty twists in this evolutionary tale.

The first is that, for reasons that aren't entirely clear, the food we really like makes us more hungry *after* we've started eating it.[12] This hyper-palatable food is, of course, loaded with all the usual health-threatening ingredients; but this second wave of hunger also seems to be related to 'priming' in the environment. If you're waiting for a friend in an Italian restaurant and you see the people at the next table digging in to an enticingly gooey four-cheese pizza, you're more likely to have problems restraining your own consumption a few minutes later. And this is true even if you weren't hungry in the first place. The need for a fix grows stronger, not weaker, as you munch your way through the pizza. You've been primed.

The second nasty twist affects people from non-Western communities that have only recently switched to a diet of processed food.

This I can illustrate from my own experience. In 2006 I found myself in a McDonald's in the middle of an Indian reservation in the south-western United States. It was a surprise to me, as an Englishman who had previously met only Americans boasting about their one-sixteenth Cherokee heritage, to discover that everyone in the restaurant appeared to be a full-blooded Native American. And I was a minority in more ways than one.

There's no polite way of saying this, but nearly every other customer was overweight. Even the teenagers working behind the till were heading towards morbid obesity. Some of them had cheeks so swollen that you could hardly see their eyes. These were Navajo adolescents, who have been shown to drink sweetened soft drinks at more than twice the national average.[13]

It was sad to see young people clearly in need of drastic intervention. And that clearly wasn't going to happen. Obesity was the norm in their community. Why? Fat people are often quick to blame their problem on their genes. This is usually self-deluding nonsense – but not in the case of these Native Americans, for whom genetic inheritance really is partly to blame.

The psychiatrist Peter Whybrow, director of the Semel Institute for Neuroscience and Human Behavior at UCLA, explains that ethnic groups with a successful history of surviving during times of scarcity are the ones that suffer most from today's biological-environmental mismatch.[14] The peoples who migrated to America's south-western deserts were forced to sustain themselves on the occasional rabbit, plus insects, roots, berries, seeds and nuts. Eventually they learned to irrigate land and grow pumpkins, corn and beans – but starvation was always a danger. Their survival was a triumph, given the environment.

But if, over many generations, a community becomes genetically adapted to scarcity, that means that when its diet suddenly changes, genetic inheritance becomes a liability.

If the percentage of your calories you derive from fat jumps from 15 to 40 per cent almost overnight, you're in trouble – particularly if this coincides with an equally sudden increase in your sugar intake and a switch to a sedentary lifestyle.

Whybrow tells the story of the Pima Indians of Arizona, who suffer from extraordinary levels of obesity and diabetes: 'Today, save for the isolated Nauru Islanders in the West Pacific, the Pima nation is plagued by a higher rate of obesity than any other ethnic group in the world, with about half those who are over the age of 35 suffering the dangerous complication of insulin-resistant diabetes.'[15]

Also, Pima children born to mothers with diabetes are at greater risk of developing it themselves. 'A disabling illness, initiated by the disruption of an ancient balance, has now become self-perpetuating within the reproductive cycle,' says Whybrow.

Similar problems, only slightly less severe in their impact, are being felt across the developing world. The Chinese government is horrified by what is happening to children who live in cities: nearly a quarter of 10- to 12-year-olds are overweight or obese, according to Education Ministry data – and most of this change has happened in the space of a decade.[16] In Brazil, former health minister José Gomes Temparão says that 'half the population is overweight', thanks to drastic changes in lifestyle and diet. In fact, exactly 50 per cent of Brazilian men are overweight. In 1990 the figure was 20 per cent.[17] Brazilians are not yet as obese as Americans, but the rate in the increase of their weight is astonishingly fast. It's as if the country's citizens have been changing shape in front of our eyes. Experts now talk about the 'nutrition transition', in which populations in developing countries move straight from malnourishment to obesity.

This might seem a melodramatic thing to say, but such rapid changes in body shape are unprecedented in the history of the world.

Genetics are an important part of the picture: anyone whose ancestors have eaten simply for thousands of years is likely to have special problems adapting to buckets of Kentucky Fried Chicken.

We in the West haven't had a sudden dietary culture shock. We've had generations in which to accommodate ourselves to diets high in sugar, fat and dairy products (to which we were originally intolerant, as most Asians are today). Even so, look where we are now: the average American woman now weighs roughly what the average American man weighed in 1960.

We also have no idea how much further this trend will continue. Nor do we really know how to go about changing our food environment in order to make it safer. Anti-smoking activists have an advantage over nutritional reformers, in that at least everyone knows what a cigarette is and that it's bad for you. There's no consensus about the boundary between healthy and unhealthy food. As Dimbleby says, most 'healthy options' in supermarkets just replace fat with sugar; given sugar's special addictive potential, they're probably making the situation worse.

'A segment of the population seems especially vulnerable to the stimuli that lead to conditioned hypereating,' concludes Kessler. 'But in the end this is behaviour that anyone can develop. Learning to overeat is an incremental process that grows with repeated exposure.'[18] Treating yourself becomes part of your daily food routine. Before long, if you ask the barista not to spray aerated cream on top of a coffee that's already got 300 calories in it, you feel that you've punished yourself.

WHY CAKE IS THE NEW COKE

Where once people responded unconsciously to food cues, they now make conscious decisions *not* to respond, thereby feeling virtuous and deprived at the same time. And nobody can keep that up for long. Walking down a modern high street resembles nothing so much as the arcade games of the 1990s, in which assailants leap out at you from behind doors and shopfronts every few seconds. Only now the assailants aren't burly mafia hit men – they're artfully packaged snacks. Is it any wonder that the crowd of grazers at Victoria Station is growing larger by the week?

6
HAPPY HOUR

Binge drinking has become one of the great health anxieties of our age – and a public nuisance that makes newspaper readers quiver with indignation. Every few months, a tabloid runs a double-page spread on 'Binge-drinking Britain', accompanied by pictures of young people vomiting, throwing punches and smashing windows after they've toppled out of a town-centre nightclub. And that's just the women.

Over the last 20 years, a combination of factors, including a drastic relaxation of licensing laws, has created new patterns of public drunkenness among drinkers in their teens and twenties.

As this crisis unfolded, the media developed a fascination with the phenomenon of 'ladettes' – brawling or comatose girls who behaved like boys after a night spent tossing back vodka shots. Newspapers that once printed blurred photographs of female binge drinkers now have websites that link to video footage of girls waving their breasts at the camera or furiously clawing at each other's frocks in sordid late-night catfights. And should viewers wish to explore this phenomenon in more depth, there's enough footage on the internet to keep them occupied for hours.

But 'ladette' is now a rather dated term. It belongs to the 1990s, when the behaviour of these young women had more shock value than it does now. That doesn't mean that ladette-style behaviour is less of a problem than it was: rather, we're just more used to it, and take it for granted that if we see a crowd of students stumbling through a town centre the girls will be as wasted as the boys.

Some YouTube videos seem to be aimed at men turned on by the sight of 'fit' girls who are blind drunk. One video is entitled: 'Young woman drunk in McDonald's (Inverness)'. It shows two teenage girls dragging a third girl, very pretty but insensible with drink, across the floor of the restaurant and down the stairs. In broad daylight. It has been watched over a million times, which is creepy when you consider how vulnerable the girl must have been to rape.

Other, less disturbing, YouTube clips extract comic value from female binge-drinking. They present it as a spectator sport, like watching women mud-wrestle (something these girls might be good at, judging by their hair-trigger tempers). Some films set the women's antics to music; others put the film on a loop, so you can watch the same girl fall over or throw up to your heart's content. But, as I say, the novelty value has worn off since the heyday of what you might call the 'ladette panic' of a few years ago, in which drunken women came to symbolise public anxieties in much the same way as the drink-sodden prostitutes of *Gin Lane*.

The really interesting question is what has happened to the original ladettes, now married or divorced women in their mid to late thirties. Some of them, at least, need little encouragement to slip back into their old ways. For a cautionary tale of what happens when a middle-class woman overdoes it, let me refer you to a sliver of CCTV footage released to newspaper websites in 2011 by British Transport Police as a warning against drinking too much over Christmas.

In the words of the *Daily Telegraph*: 'The cringeworthy footage shows the elegantly dressed woman appearing more than a little worse for wear as she alights from the late-night train at Barnsley station, South Yorks.

'Wearing a hat, dress and what look to be flat shoes, she staggers off the carriage of the Northern service before violently lurching to her right and tumbling over. Throwing out an arm to support herself against the side of the train, she is unable to prevent her rapid descent and collapses on the ground before rolling off the platform.

'The clip ends with the woman completely out of sight as she lies trapped between the train and the platform.'[1]

We can tell from the light-hearted tone of the report that the woman was unharmed, aside from a few cuts and bruises. The police had made the film public with the woman's permission.

But if they thought the film would serve as a warning against alcohol, they were being naive. Instead, it went viral. Why was it so popular? Not because people found it scary, but because they found it so funny. But would the video have been such a hit if it had featured a man rather than a woman? I doubt it. Much of the humour (and here I must come clean: I did chuckle) derives from the sight of a neatly dressed lady toppling backwards and then turning over like a rolling pin before disappearing from sight.

The newspapers had more fun in June 2011, accusing middle-aged women of behaving like football hooligans when the 1990s boy band Take That visited Manchester and Cardiff for reunion concerts. As the *Daily Mail* reported, with unconcealed relish:

> They arrived in their thousands, leaving their husbands and children at home and ready to relive their teenage past. But the excitement of seeing their idols in concert proved too much for hordes of Take That fans of a certain age.
>
> More than 100 women were admitted to hospital after marathon drinking sessions and alcohol-fuelled brawls before the one-time boy band took to the stage.
>
> The fans' antics led to them being branded worse than drunken football hooligans. But they did win praise from Take That singer Robbie Williams, who is now teetotal following a long battle with drink and drugs.
>
> 'We used to have the record for the number of girls fainting,' the 37-year-old told the crowd at their concert in Cardiff on Wednesday night. 'Now we have the record for the most middle-aged boozed-up women. I, Robbie Williams, am proud of you.'[2]

The superannuated Take That fans were mainly working-class, but they certainly included a fair number of middle-class women who had smuggled vodka into the concert. It was no isolated incident. Suburban women are discreetly engaging in heavy drinking sessions – though the extent of their boozing is disguised by bars and restaurants with goblet-shaped glasses that hold nearly half a pint of white wine. This is quite deliberate policy on the part of wine bars: the owners know that women feel less self-conscious about putting back 'two or three glasses' than a whole bottle, even if they end up drinking the same amount.

I'm sorry if my concentration on women binge-drinking seems sexist: no one is suggesting that they drink more or behave worse than their male partners, many of whom are extending their adolescent drinking patterns into early middle age. But it's the social change that people have noticed. In fact, it's the one that I've noticed, again and again. Two girls who were friends of mine when they were in their early twenties are now married with children and hose down the Chablis on their evenings in. I shouldn't extrapolate from that, but I've also noticed the increased presence of women at AA meetings.

In Britain, there has been a rapid narrowing of the alcohol gender gap.[3] Research from the Joseph Rowntree Foundation found that binge drinking among women rose from eight per cent in 1998 to 15 per cent in 2006 – that is, almost doubled. Over the same period, male binge drinking increased only slightly, from 22 to 23 per cent. Note that these statistics aren't restricted to 'ladettes': they refer to women of all ages. To spell it out: women are now exposed to changes in brain chemistry that had previously been restricted to men.

In America, too, there is anxiety about what *Salon* magazine calls 'the trend of lady bingers'.[4] According to the US National Women's Law Center's statistics for 2010, 10.6 per cent of women had sunk five or more drinks on at least one occasion in the past month.[5] In England, the number of women drinking more than six units of alcohol on one occasion in the previous week (the NHS measure of bingeing – it's eight units for men) was 15 per cent in 2006.[6]

These figures aren't really comparable, since their methodology is so different – but the impression that British women binge drink more than American women is probably correct. Also, one has only to compare the YouTube videos to see that British girls get drunk in a different way from their US counterparts – that is, they're far more likely to do so in plain view of others.

There's a simple reason for this. In both cases, women are copying national male drinking habits. America has a taboo against public drunkenness that dates back to its puritan origins; Britain, on the other hand, has until recently extended reluctant tolerance to noisy drunks at closing time. It's no accident that American videos show girls bouncing off the walls of their rooms, whereas there are countless clips of British women singing drunkenly in the street.

Despite these cultural differences, however, the 'alcohol gender gap' has been closing on both sides of the Atlantic – for mature women as well as for girls. American and British professional women no longer feel embarrassed about knocking back a few drinks after work. The cheeky cocktail culture depicted in *Sex and the City* is found in all major US cities and has spread to Britain.

The health consequences of this are serious. It's not sexist to point out that women process alcohol less efficiently than men. To quote the US journalist Tracy Clark-Flory, 'I've boasted that I could drink my male friends under the table, and I have at times through sheer force of will. Not even my iron will can force my liver to process booze differently, though.'[7]

●

When I was a drinker, I didn't know many women with drink problems. Some of them threw up from time to time, but that was only to be expected. In the 1980s, young men and women tended not to go on binges together: the girls made their excuses and left as soon as the boys started boring them senseless with drunken boasting. Then again, perhaps the women were there and I just don't remember them. Those years are distinctly soft-focus – which is a blessing, all things considered.

I also can't remember when my binges turned into alcoholism. Maybe that's because, for a very long time, they were the same thing. As I'm typing these words, I keep stopping to try to work out when my drinking got the better of me. But it's tricky: I can't distinguish between losing control of myself in the sense that everyone does when they're intoxicated and losing control of my life because I was perpetually drunk and hung over.

HAPPY HOUR

I've heard many people in AA meetings announce that 'alcohol was a liberation from my unhappy childhood'. I can relate to that. For me, booze was more like a tantalisingly short day pass from the prison I had constructed with my own behaviour.

I was one of those children whose natural curiosity was easily smothered by natural laziness. The town of Reading in the late 1970s was not a stimulating environment. My school, Presentation College, was run by Irish brothers whose real religion was football, a sport I loathed. Fortunately, some of my teachers were cut from a different mould: these were men whose intellectual exuberance was matched only by their fondness for alcohol. They became my friends; they still are. When I was in the sixth form, they took me to very ordinary pubs – there was no other sort in Reading – for what were, by my standards, riotously funny evenings in which I drank between three and five pints of lager. Crisps were consumed. Peanuts, too. It was heavenly.

It says something about my lack of self-awareness that not once during those sessions, or for years afterwards, did I notice that I was using lager to change my mood. But it's not as if the clues weren't there.

When I was in the pub with my school friends, I would get ratty if the pace of round-buying was slowed by leisurely drinkers. I had to fall back on a trick passed on to me, with quasi-masonic solemnity, by my geography teacher: 'inter-round drinks' – that is, a quick half pint or a whisky chaser bought surreptitiously on the way back from the loo.

Another clue: if, by any chance, the landlord of a pub decided to carry on serving alcohol after the cruelly early closing time of

10.30 p.m., my excitement was uncontainable. It was all I could do to stop myself falling at the feet of old Len Crook of the Spread Eagle. You'd think I was a convict whose life had just been spared by a magnanimous ruler. The extra two or three pints weren't especially enjoyable: the peak of pleasure always came earlier in the evening, somewhere around the second pint. But, to use Kent Berridge's terminology, my 'wanting' had continued to intensify even while the 'liking' levelled off.

I didn't take a gap year; grammar school boys rarely did in 1980. If I had, perhaps I would have been better prepared for Oxford. My college, Mansfield, was small and unpretentious. God knows how I would have coped at Christ Church or Magdalen, but even so I was terrified. I discovered reserves of shyness that I didn't know I possessed. Too nervous to talk to the other students in my college, I headed straight for the only place I'd visited as a sixth former, the Oxford Union. Debate nights offered an ideal opportunity to self-medicate with alcohol. They seemed to attract every lonely show-off in the university.

To cut a long story short, I fell in with a crowd who binge drank out of social insecurity. We didn't call it binge drinking, of course, and none of us admitted to feelings of inferiority, though we enjoyed drawing attention to each other's hang-ups.

Only one of us had been to a major public school. Simon was a charming, feckless and foggy-headed Etonian who, stuck in a minor college and from a penniless family, basked in our sycophancy rather than trying to gain entry to the tightly policed dining societies run by the Old Etonian elite. He was also an uncompromising boozer. You drank until you fell over – and no complaints the next day. Hangovers were 'common'.

Thank God he was away serving in the Army when I attended his sister's 21st birthday party and threw up into his grandmother's handbag.

Social insecurity isn't often cited as a factor in binge drinking, but perhaps it should be. I'm thinking especially of the misery that comes from finding yourself surrounded by smart people you want to emulate. Oxford in the early 1980s was full of undergraduates from modest backgrounds trying to 'pass', as they used to say in the Deep South. (I can recall only one boy from an unglamorous day school who, thanks to his spectacular good looks, did break into Oxford high society, and that was the future actor then known as 'Hughie' Grant.)

This was the heyday of the Sloane Ranger – and the fake Sloane Ranger, recognisable by his suspiciously clean Barbour oilskin jacket and chain-store brogues. Maybe this is just my impression, but the fakes, of whom I was one, seemed to be more extravagant drunks than the real thing. There was a pathetic quality to our all-night benders. We were acting a role, none too convincingly.

Although we'd got into Oxford, our fogeyish high jinks remind me a bit of the sad mock-*Brideshead* antics of dining clubs at redbrick universities. We stole traffic cones and set off fire extinguishers in feeble imitations of the practised horseplay of boys brought up on country estates. I don't recall meeting a single member of the Bullingdon Club in three years – but if I had, I have a horrible suspicion I'd have asked for his autograph.

How many of us turned into alcoholics? It's difficult to say. For some, heavy drinking was a phase. Others remained locked into the pattern of bingeing that they laid down for themselves when they were at university.

A study of 600 Finnish twins published in the journal *Alcoholism: Clinical and Environmental Research* in 2011 found that drinking problems at 16 'robustly predict alcohol diagnoses' at 25.[8] It certainly predicted mine, though I waited until the age of 32 before announcing, 'My name's Damian and I'm an alcoholic.'

I arrived in Fleet Street in 1989, paying virtually no rent and with a fat expense account. Even by the standards of young journalists, I was a flamboyant drunk. In those days the satirical magazine *Private Eye* gave an honourable mention to the drunkest person at their very crowded and boozy annual party. I shouldn't be proud, though of course I am, of the fact that I won it in 1992. And this when I was the religious affairs correspondent of a national newspaper. (To put that in perspective, I should point out that my best professional contacts – the so-called 'gin, lace and backbiting' fraternity of High Anglican priests – could have drunk most politicians under the table. Some of them even conducted Communion services while inebriated; one wonders how Archbishop Cranmer would have reacted to hearing his stately prose delivered in a drunken slur.)

HAPPY HOUR

By the age of 30, I'd started doing something I swore I'd never do: drinking on my own. To my surprise, I discovered that sitting at home with a bottle of red wine wasn't a lonely business. On the contrary, it was – or seemed to be – a cure for loneliness. This was my way of replacing people by things. At the time I didn't grasp that the substance had taken the place of my old friends – in other words, that I was sliding towards addiction in the most predictable manner. In my experience, all addicts think of themselves as special cases. It's only recently that I've come to think of myself as a fairly typical casualty of an environment saturated with my drug of choice. But at some level I did come to think of red wine as congenial company – that is, until it ran out, a situation I learned to avoid by buying two bottles from Oddbins on my way home from work. And if I felt the need to talk, there was always the telephone.

'Drunk dialling' is one of the worst ordeals that loquacious drunks can inflict on their friends, and I was an absolute menace. Thank God email wasn't around. Or Twitter, the perfect platform for drunks sitting at home with a bottle of claret who feel the urge to curse like fishwives or deliver a maudlin confession to the world that they will reread in horror the next morning. The thought of it makes my blood run cold.

One morning in 1992 I woke up in a strange bed, alone in a strange house. I had to tiptoe into the drawing room and check the family photographs on the mantelpiece to work out which kind soul had taken me in. That was the sort of thing that happened to me all the time. But I never got used to the chaos; at some level I was deeply ashamed.

What I hated in particular was the unpredictable quality of my drinking. In the words of the AA saying I quoted earlier, I was one of those alcoholics who say to themselves: 'I'm going to the pub tonight and I *won't* get totally smashed.' And sometimes I didn't.

But the evenings when, by some fluke, I managed to stay relatively sober were becoming rarer and rarer. Three or four mornings a week, I would ring my closest woman friend, Cristina Odone, the mini-skirted Italian editor of the *Catholic Herald*. 'I did it again,' I would say. 'Madonna!' she would sigh.

Cristina wasn't a drinker, but Clare (not her real name), another women I greatly respected, was in the AA fellowship and had quietly made it clear that if I ever wanted to try it out, she'd take me to a meeting.

On 15 April 1994, I rang Cristina and confessed to a disastrous binge which had begun, implausibly, over lunch with a heavy-drinking aide to the Archbishop of Canterbury and taken me all over the West End. Don't ask me where; I have no idea. That I ended up in my own bed, alone, was a miracle. I rang the *Catholic Herald*.

Cristina said: 'Either you call Clare, or I do. Which is it to be?'

I called Clare.

•

Recently I was talking to a psychiatrist at a teaching hospital attached to London University. He asked me about my university drinking and, since he's an old friend, I told him frankly that I'd belonged to a circle of unhappy pissheads who were looked on with pity by other students. 'We were very much in a minority, and we knew it,' I added.

'Well, you certainly wouldn't be in a minority now,' he said.

No one could deny that students are more vigorous binge drinkers than they were a generation ago. The explanation for this lies in the convergence of the different types of availability.

The simultaneous weakening of the taboos against women drinking and against extreme drinking in public has been methodically exploited by alcohol manufacturers. As a report by the think-tank Demos observes: 'The landscape of the night-time economy has obviously grown around existing demand, but sometimes supply can create demand. In other words, when young people go out into this landscape they are to some extent encouraged to indulge in reckless intoxicated behaviour, because that is what the landscape has been set up to do.'[9] Bar crawling doesn't involve much time-consuming travel: the next port of call is just a couple of doors away.

Supermarkets, too, have contributed hugely to the economic availability of alcohol. They sell wine, beer and spirits as loss-leaders. That's one of the main reasons alcohol was 69.4 per cent more affordable in 2007 than it was in 1980.[10]

Clearly there's some sort of social epidemic going on. Drinks manufacturers benefit from it, but there are other considerations that have nothing to do with profit margins. University students are placing greater stress on binge drinking as a social bonding exercise. We can see the alcohol gender gap closing with a vengeance on campuses all over the UK. If the British government meets its ridiculous target of sending 50 per cent of all young people to university, then it had better prepare for a sharp increase in the number of alcoholic casualties – especially among women whose bodies are constitutionally ill-suited to bingeing.

But binge drinking isn't only a British problem, or an American one; it's spreading to countries which have never had a tradition of public drunkenness – which have regarded such behaviour as a source of shame, indeed.

Just as southern European countries were protected from high rates of heart disease by the fabled 'Mediterranean diet', so their patterns of alcohol consumption ruled out the boozy street theatre so familiar to Britons. The French, admittedly, drank wine with a relentlessness that endangered their livers, but the steady pace meant that their intoxication didn't draw attention to itself. As for Italy and Spain, alcohol was an accompaniment to food in restaurants, consumed at an inexplicably gentle pace. (I'll never be able to understand the appeal of a single glass of wine with a plate of pasta. I mean, why bother?)

This old Mediterranean pace of drinking is being challenged, however, by young Spaniards and Italians who have developed a taste for bingeing. Spain is now overrun by teenagers who sit around drinking a mixture of whisky and coke from a plastic bottle known as *el botellon*, the big bottle. By 2004 it was being reported that 44 per cent of 15- to 19-year-old boys in Spain regularly get drunk, a proportion that had doubled since the start of the decade. Only a quarter of teenage girls got drunk – but that, too, represented a doubling of the percentage.[11] The old folks are scandalised.

This trend isn't confined to Europe. The Singaporean government has declared binge drinking to be 'an emerging issue', and the local media have taken enthusiastically to illustrating it. In the words of one news report: 'He got drunk at a friend's house and ended up taking off all his clothes in the bathroom. "The next thing I knew," said student Mervyn Lee, 19, "I woke up in my friend's bed wearing a fresh pair of shorts."'[12] That might strike a Glaswegian as an unremarkable episode, something barely worth mentioning, but in a society gripped by control freakery, as Singapore is, even a teenager drunkenly misplacing his shorts is a cause for alarm.

The outbreak of Western-style drinking in east Asia has surprised the authorities, who imagined that a genetic intolerance to alcohol would protect their citizens. But many young people are prepared to put up with the embarrassment of 'Asian flush syndrome', as it's known, and the vomiting that goes with it. A British foreign correspondent who spent five years in Japan told me: 'Every time I think of Tokyo, I can smell the stench of puke on the underground. It's one of the reasons I was glad to leave.'

Young Asians aren't, of course, modelling their social lives on those of British bingers. Singaporean and British students are drawing common inspiration from the exaggerated depictions of US college partying they pick up from films and television. Even American students are trying to live up to the stereotype of hard-drinking frat houses. One US website offers a list of 'the 15 wildest partying movies' to watch during spring break, which it describes as 'the perfect time to do beer bongs on the beach, soak up the sun and cram into a dance club with date rapists and other revellers'.[13]

In America, the problem isn't that the proportion of college students who binge drink is rising: around 40 per cent of them have been doing so for a long time. The notable development is that the *frequency* of their drinking sessions is increasing. Around a quarter of students get drunk two or three times over a two-week period, whereas the figure in 2000 was under 20 per cent.[14]

This squares with my own conversations with university and school teachers in Britain. The amount young people are drinking now has as much to do with their habit of drinking more often as with the total amount they consume on any one evening. Regular 'partying' – a purely American verb until a few years ago – has replaced occasional parties; celebration has become a habit. It's true that young people have never needed encouragement to celebrate, but the ever-increasing popularity of 'themed' events at colleges means that scarcely a day goes by without an excuse to get wasted. And not just on alcohol, either.

●

No account of alcohol binges can leave pills and powders out of the picture. For partygoers, they belong to the same hedonic experience. That's a dramatic social change, and one that policymakers – who grew up when alcohol and drugs were very different things – have difficulty getting their heads around.

HAPPY HOUR

When I was at university, even smoking a joint was loaded with social significance. Plenty of people did so, but for most of them – certainly for me – it was a self-conscious, slightly thrilling, journey into the world of 'taking drugs'.

As with heavy drinking, there was an aspirational aspect to it. Dope smoking was associated with public schoolboys and especially Old Etonians. An acquaintance of mine smoked quite a few spliffs with David Cameron, the future Prime Minister. Whether Cameron tried anything harder at Oxford isn't clear, but it's interesting that, in 2012, neither the Prime Minister nor the Chancellor of the Exchequer had denied snorting cocaine. Neither, come to think of it, had the current President of the United States, nor his predecessor. One of these days someone should write a book entitled *Tory MPs Who Have Done Drugs*. It wouldn't necessarily be a slim volume. (One former MP whom I know for a fact has a nose like a vacuum cleaner recently told his local radio station he'd never touched anything stronger than alcohol.)

The arrival and instant popularity of Ecstasy in the mid 1980s did two things: it blurred the distinction between hard and soft drugs and it introduced millions of young people to the notion of a binge in the form of a pill. Ecstasy produced a more euphoric effect than alcohol – at least for the first few times – but the duration of the hit and the bleak come-down followed the trajectory of an alcoholic bender. Also, such was the social acceptability of the drug that many youngsters who previously felt no inclination to get smashed every weekend now found themselves using the products of an illegal laboratory to manipulate their moods.

Probably not one person in a thousand who takes MDMA (the active ingredient in Ecstasy) can tell you what the letters stand for. The answer is methylenedioxymethamphetamine. As the drug researchers Harvey Milkman and Stanley Sunderwirth point out, the second half of that word should be a red flag to anyone.

'Meth' is one the nastiest street drugs known to man, and its (originally) middle-class derivative Ecstasy has a similar capacity to cause long-term brain damage by overstimulating serotonin and dopamine.[15] We still don't know what price the first generation of 'E' users will pay for their quasi-religious devotion to the drug now that they're entering middle age. And what has happened in the meantime makes research far more complicated, since MDMA has seeped out of the clubs and into bars all over the world, mutating chemically as it does so. In the process, cocaine has also lost much of its mystique: coke, Ecstasy, ketamine – what you take largely depends on what's around.

Dr Max Pemberton's work as a psychiatrist in the Accident and Emergency department of a London hospital involves asking young patients about their drug and alcohol history. 'As soon as they know I'm not going to rat on them, most of them admit to doing something – coke, MDMA, mephedrone, ketamine – in the previous few days,' he says.

'What the older generation doesn't understand is that combining drugs and alcohol is *normal* for young clubbers. They might do a bit of coke before they go out, or "pre-loading" with a few drinks, then go to a bar and get drunk, do a line of coke in the loos and stop drinking. If they go on to a club they'll drop a pill – or maybe pure MDMA, because no one trusts Ecstasy these days. They don't know what's in it. The last thing they want to do then is drink and many of the clubs won't even serve alcohol anyway. Then they go back to someone's house and want to come down, so they use Zopiclone, Zolpidem or Valium.'

Is this typical behaviour for young people? 'Well, let's say the ones who aren't risk averse. They know they're doing something a bit naughty. But now that anyone can buy pills off the internet, there's isn't the same sense of personal risk. And a lot of these drugs are really, really cheap when they first appear. If it costs literally pennies to get off your face, why spend forty quid or more doing it on booze?

'I used to see long lines of kids queuing outside Fabric [a London nightclub geared towards party-hard middle-class trendies] in the early hours of the morning. It was freezing and they were only wearing T-shirts and I thought: if the police lined them up for a drugs test every single one of them would test positive. But, as I say, that sort of behaviour is normal now. It's part of taking control of your own psychopharmacology. It's about wanting everything. And it's not going away.'

Indeed. New clubbing drugs are emerging almost every week. In 2010 alone, 40 new substances were released on to UK streets – nearly all of them 'legal highs'. All that means is that the Government hadn't caught up with them yet. As it is, there are now over 600 substances controlled under the Misuse of Drugs Act.

The internet, inevitably, is accelerating the dissemination of these substances. As they say in the tech start-up community, e-commerce is infinitely scalable: websites selling drugs can serve as many customers as their owners have supplies to satisfy. There's no need to recruit an army of street dealers when you've got a PayPal-enabled web page. The sheer speed of this process means that toxicologists don't have time to analyse the short-term and long-term effects of such drugs. With an almost incredible disregard for their health, clubbers are happily swallowing pills with names like Roflcopter before anyone knows exactly what's in them – apart, of course, from the rogue chemists who have just cooked them up.

Government scientists are scrambling desperately to classify these drugs and warn young people of the dangers of taking them. But the underground laboratories, and their new digital sales departments, are too far ahead. It's a lost cause.

In any case, declaring war on drugs is a rather old-fashioned thing to do these days. When young people get wasted, it's not just on drugs but on drugs, alcohol, *whatever*. The hedonic experience involves whatever you can get your hands on or whatever feels right at the time. Many binges involve planned sequences of drinks and drugs that are intended to sketch the trajectory of their experience. We may never reach the stage where, after dropping a bottle of vodka into the supermarket trolley, a clubber thinks, 'Oh, mustn't forget the MDMA,' and reaches up for a packet. But the stuff is only a phone call away, so what's the difference?

7
DRUGSTORE
COWBOYS

The use and abuse of prescription drugs in America has to be seen to be believed. Some people are addicted to painkillers; others are stealing medication as a desperate form of recreation; an alarming number, including children, are trying to boost their academic performance with amphetamines innocently packaged as cognitive enhancers.

At any rate, for millions of US citizens, ranging from seniors in Miami retirement homes to seniors at Harvard Law, those bottles of pills have become a way of life. It's a problem in Britain, too. In fact, it's been a problem for me. But first let me tell you about my encounters with the prescription drug subculture in California.

My friend Tim earns a living setting off fireworks. He's one of the most skilled and fearless pyrotechnicians on the West Coast. He has also been diagnosed with Attention Deficit Hyperactivity Disorder (ADHD), for which he is treated with the amphetamine-based drug Adderall. ADHD is a dangerous condition to have if you rely on split-second judgements while running between giant fireworks that could fry off your face if your attention wanders. Adderall allows you to summon up mighty reserves of concentration. So it would seem to be in everybody's interests for Tim's perfectly legal prescriptions to be dispensed by pharmacies.

But there's a problem. It's difficult to get a prescription for Adderall filled in California. This I know, because one day in October 2011, Tim and I drove round a dozen pharmacies in East LA, only to be met with frowns and theatrical shrugs as soon as the staff saw what the script was for.

If you've never visited a US drugstore, imagine a full-sized super-market stocked with reading glasses, vitamin supplements, cut-price toiletries and hair-loss products – plus a pharmacy section that looks like the reception desk of a hospital.

To say that Tim hates pharmacists is an understatement. 'Think of Kafka, with the punitive snarl of the prosecuting magistrate replaced by the passive-aggressive smile of a "friendly" pharmacist whose teeth are too white to trust,' he says.

'You'd assume that picking up a legal medication prescribed to you from a doctor with a wall full of degree certificates would be a snap, particularly when you consider that it costs nearly $400. But no. These lab-coated "professionals" specialise in what I call sponta-neous legislation – that is, their own bullshit excuses for refusing to serve you.'

I sympathise. Over the years, I've had run-ins of my own with Boots pharmacists who behave like professors of medicine. (Hint for those on the receiving end of their pomposity: 'It's not my fault you didn't get into med school' is a good parting shot.) But I've never encountered the sort of difficulties we had that day.

Tim and I wasted five hours visiting pharmacies in Glendale, Eagle Rock and Pasadena trying to get his Adderall. The excuse in nearly every store was the same: the whole county of Los Angeles was running low on the drug. Tim didn't believe them, and spent the night cold-calling pharmacies. No luck. It put him in a foul mood. Despite his protestations that Adderall simply restores him to normality, Tim does like the stuff. His postdated prescription had suddenly become valid and, like the sugar-chasing snackers we met in Chapter 5, he was experiencing the chemical rush of anticipation. His script was a powerful cue – only it wasn't delivering.

By this stage he was convinced that there was some sort of conspiracy against him. As it turns out, however, all those unhelpful pharmacists were telling the truth. They couldn't have given Tim the drug even if they'd wanted to.

In January 2012, ABC news ran a story on the chronic shortage of Adderall. Apparently, patients all over the country were having the same experience in drugstores. The report included some scary statistics: as of 2007, 5.4 million US schoolchildren had been diagnosed with ADD (attention deficit disorder without the hyperactivity) or ADHD – that's nearly 10 per cent of children in the country. A total of 18 million Adderall prescriptions were written in 2010, an increase of 13.4 per cent since 2009.

'As demand for the drug grows, more and more patients have found the medication is out of stock at local pharmacies,' said the report. 'Experts say it's difficult to say where the reason for the drug shortage lies.'[1]

That seems rather naive of the experts. As Tim says, Adderall is one of those medications that can put a smile on your face. It is, after all, a powerful psychostimulant made from amphetamine salts. Basically, it's a sort of slow-release speed.

The Drug Enforcement Agency is deeply suspicious of its popularity and has imposed quotas on the amount drug companies can manufacture. Those quotas are supposed to meet the legitimate demand for Adderall – but demand for it extends way beyond people with rock-solid diagnoses of ADD or ADHD, to include millions of consumers whose 'attention deficit' is little more than creative self-diagnosis, happily accepted by gullible doctors. In January 2012, the actress Demi Moore suffered a seizure apparently brought on by a combination of self-starvation and Adderall – which, among other things, is a powerful appetite suppressant.[2]

Let me tell you about the time I took Adderall.

I was staying with a hospital consultant and his attorney wife in the East Bay just outside San Francisco. I'd driven overnight from Los Angeles after a flight from London; I was jetlagged, sleep-deprived and facing a deadline to write an article for the *Spectator* about, of all things, Bach cantatas.

Sitting in the courtyard garden with my laptop, I tapped and deleted one clumsy sentence after another. The sun was going down;

my hostess saw me shivering and popped out with a blanket, a cup of herbal tea and 'something to help you concentrate'.

I took the pill, didn't notice any effect, and was glad when I was called in for dinner.

The dining room was a Californian take on the Second Empire. The lady next to me was a Southern Belle turned realtor, her eyelids already drooping from the effects of her third giant glass of Napa Valley chardonnay. She began to tell me about her divorce. Every time she refilled her glass, her new husband raised his eyes to heaven.

It felt as if I was stuck in an episode of *Dallas*, or a very bad Tennessee Williams play. But it didn't matter in the least because, at some stage between the mozzarella salad and the grilled chicken, I'd become as high as a kite.

Adderall helps you concentrate, no doubt about it. I was *riveted* by the details of this woman's alimony settlement. Even she, utterly self-obsessed as she was, was surprised by my gushing empathy. After dinner, I sat down at the kitchen table to finish the article. The head rush was beginning to wear off, but then, just as I started typing, a second wave of amphetamine pushed its way into my bloodstream. This was timed-release Adderall. Gratefully I plunged into 18th-century Leipzig, meticulously noting the catalogue numbers of cantatas. It was as if the great Johann Sebastian himself was looking over my shoulder. By the time I glanced at the clock, it was five in the morning. My pleasure at finishing the article was boosted by the dopamine high. What a lovely drug.

The blues didn't hit me until the next day – and took the best part of a week to banish.

And this is what they give to restless nine-year-olds. Defenders of the practice say kids with attention deficit who take Adderall and Ritalin, another amphetamine-based stimulant, are given the gift of concentration *without the potentially addictive high*. They don't experience the chemical thrill I felt because their brain deficiency cancels out the chemical thrill I experienced.

I've always been suspicious of this argument, so I was interested to read, in January 2012, an article in the *New York Times* by L. Alan Sroufe, a retired professor of child psychology who has closely monitored the pharmaceutical treatment of children with ADD for over 30 years. Sroufe now believes that millions of children diagnosed with ADD are being treated for brain abnormalities that they don't actually have – that their genuine behavioural problems, which like all behaviour are governed by the brain, are often induced by environmental factors.

Yes, Adderall and Ritalin calmed them down in the classroom. But, said Sroufe, the drugs have the same effect on *all* children, not just those diagnosed with attention deficit.

Also, like anyone else who takes stimulant drugs, these children develop a tolerance to them. As he put it: 'Many parents who take their children off the drugs find that behaviour worsens, which most likely confirms their belief that the drugs work. But the behaviour worsens because the children's bodies have become adapted to the drug. Adults may have similar reactions if they suddenly cut back on coffee, or stop smoking.'[3]

One can't help suspecting that the children themselves worked out most of this a long time ago. They know Adderall and Ritalin can be used to get high. That's why some of them claim to have ADD or ADHD: the symptoms aren't exactly hard to fake, after all. And that's why some kids with legitimate prescriptions are happy to sell their pills to classmates – or to let their mother or father 'borrow' a few. Older siblings, too, like to get hold of these drugs: what could be nicer than a mellow form of speed that enhances the experience of video games and sex?

The naivety of American doctors when it comes to prescribing Adderall and Ritalin is a constant source of astonishment to their British colleagues. Let's take the case of another American friend of mine, Patrick. He exhibits the symptoms of attention deficit disorder in abundance – alternately daydreaming and rushing off on wild errands, losing his drift in the middle of sentences, shifting and squirming in his seat until his eyes alight on a new object over which he can obsess.

Patrick had no difficulty persuading a string of doctors that he needed Adderall, which he said was the only drug that allowed him to concentrate on his office job. That's not the whole story, though. Patrick spent his mid thirties addicted to crystal meth. He's been clean for a couple of years, which is miraculous – but this is absolutely no guarantee that he'll *stay* clean.

Crystal meth, or methamphetamine, has been described as dopamine's evil twin. The dopamine it produces is thought to be 600 times the normal amount of the chemical the brain releases during pleasurable events. Users binge, crash, fall into a fitful slumber, then often start again. Weight loss is dramatic – which is cool at first, but not so cool when you became so malnourished that you start looking like a toothless 90-year-old. Which is what Patrick resembled, judging by the Facebook photographs worried friends sent me during the worst of his addiction. At one stage even his mother told me she was resigned to him dying.

Here's what I find incredible. Every single American doctor who wrote Patrick prescriptions for amphetamine drugs for his ADHD, or supposed ADHD, knew he was a former meth addict. Don't ask me what was going through their minds. 'Attention deficit' has a quasi-mythical status in the US that seems to override the medical profession's common sense. Also, Patrick is a brilliant talker, and maybe he managed to deflect the doctors' attention away from evidence of multiple drug rehab sessions on his medical records.

At any rate, I'm pretty certain that no honest British GP would hand out a prescription for amphetamines to a man who has been brought to the brink of death by crystal meth. Just to check, I asked one of my oldest friends, a family doctor in the Midlands, whether he would have given Patrick the drug. 'Are you kidding?' he asked. 'I don't prescribe that shit for *anything*.'

Patrick's story illustrates how chaotic the prescribing of mood-altering drugs has become in the United States. In 2004 six million

Americans admitted to non-medical use of prescription drugs – that's 2.5 per cent of the population.[4] Many of them were doing so for understandable reasons. For example, it's hard to blame an old lady who's given Vicodin for a twisted ankle if she carries on using the drug even after pain disappears; it may be the only thing that lifts her mood since her husband died. And if a husband 'borrows' his wife's Valium when his nerves are shot to pieces by a round of redundancies in his office, is that a hanging offence?

A codeine addict who is prescribed the medicine for arthritis explained to me: 'I find it hard to tell when the pain relief ends and you're simply enjoying the medicine. Let's just say that, while it doesn't get you very high, it makes the furniture really comfortable.'

One is inclined to be less sympathetic, however, if a college student raids his room-mate's (legal) supply of Ritalin to get him through an essay crisis – and even less so if, after an all-night cocaine binge, he calms down his central nervous system with Xanax ordered through the internet.

What we're confronting here goes further than a blurring of the boundary between legal and illegal drugs. Also evaporating are the distinctions between the legal, inappropriate and unlawful use of medicines, plus the difference between medication and self-medication.

The problem is nicely illustrated by an anonymous question submitted to a website where lawyers answer readers' queries. Someone, presumably a young male, had been caught with nine

Adderall pills without prescription. The lawyer's advice? Quick – find a doctor who will diagnose you with ADHD and give you the drug *before* the case comes to court, and then you could find your offence downgraded from a felony to a misdemeanour.[5]

That trick wouldn't work in Britain: our doctors aren't so easily manipulated, at least in this area. But, as we shall see later, Adderall and the addictive problems associated with it are already an everyday part of life on the campuses of Britain's elite universities. And the authorities haven't a clue what to do about it.

•

There is no experience quite like dropping a tranquilliser on top of a vicious, late-stage hangover. I'm thinking of the point at which the headache has disappeared, but your muscles are aching, you're disorientated from lack of sleep and you feel morbidly guilty about what you've done to yourself. Again.

I actually used to look forward to arriving at that pitch of discomfort, because that was when I could reach for the blister pack of Zimovane, a trade name for the relatively new sleeping pill zopiclone, and push out two oval-shaped 7.5 mg pills, twice the prescribed dose.

Zopiclone, like other tranquillisers and sleeping pills, suppresses the central nervous system. Its chemical profile is very similar to those of benzodiazepine drugs such as diazepam (Valium), though the experience of taking it is quite different. It isn't one of those drugs that creep up on you; it suddenly announces its presence by changing the visual texture of the world around you. No amount of photoshopping could recreate the effect, and it's not easy to put into words. But let's suppose I was wearing a woolly sweater. It would look … woollier. My coffee table would look more woody. And as I stepped through this pharmaceutical looking glass, my hangover would melt away.

So, alas, would my inhibitions. Zopiclone didn't put silly, giggly thoughts into my head, like marijuana; nor did it produce the egocentric monologues you hear from cocaine users. It was worse than that.

Far from sending me to sleep, this sleeping pill would persuade me to say the most stupid, inappropriate thing that came into my head. The only consolation is that no drug empties the memory bank more thoroughly. So I have only the dimmest recollection of being in the Groucho Club, then the most fashionable media venue in London, at the same time as Robbie Coltrane, the Scottish actor best known for his starring role in the crime series *Cracker* and for playing Hagrid in the Harry Potter films. This was 1993, by which point in his career Coltrane was already alarmingly fat. It's a topic he famously hates talking about. In interviews he has declared his weight to be 'a taboo subject' – but there's no such thing as a taboo when you've just washed down 15 mg of zopiclone with a vodka and tonic.

According to the friend who was with me, I did the one thing guaranteed to cause even more offence than teasing Coltrane about his weight: I went up to him and *congratulated him on coming to terms with his fatness.*

I've occasionally asked my friend what happened next. 'You really don't want to know,' he replies. 'Let's just say you made the most complete and utter prat of yourself.'

Soon afterwards, I gave up alcohol. It was a relatively straightforward business: the stuff had beaten me and I never wanted to touch it again. But the insidious habit of self-medicating with tranquillisers proved more difficult to kick.

In the summer of 1994, a couple of months into my so-called sobriety, my AA sponsor, an Anglican clergyman, told me firmly to stay off the zopiclone. I must have sounded surprised, because he went on: 'Don't you remember ringing me last night?' I didn't.

'Then you won't remember asking me how I reconciled being married with being secretly gay.'

Does zopiclone mess with other people's brains in the same humiliating fashion? Most people use it as intended – that is, by taking it just before getting into bed – so you don't hear many accounts of its strange properties. But a few years ago I did come across a report of one normally reticent old lady who, having taken her pills, rang up her friends to regale them with jolly stories about her late husband's infidelities. They were mortified on her behalf. She had no recollection of the conversations.

My abuse of zopiclone wasn't reinforced by my friendships, as my drinking had been. In fact, my friends dreaded hearing me ramble on under its influence. Sometimes I would try to conceal the fact that I'd dropped a tablet – but the drug always gave me away, not just because

I talked drivel but because it made me trip over my words in a distinctive fashion.

This was a late stage in my addiction to alcohol, by which time most of my relationships were in ruins anyway and I was busily replacing people by things. So I don't think it's a coincidence that I developed a ritualised relationship with zopiclone pills. There must have been an almighty dopamine rush when the chemist handed me that paper bag of goodies – not unlike the thrill the compulsive shopper feels when a credit card payment goes through. And I know that, from the moment I had the pills in my pocket, I was already planning what was, in effect, the ceremony of taking them.

These solitary rituals usually happened the night after a crippling alcohol binge. I would starve myself during the day – I was too hung over to eat, anyway – in preparation for the 15 mg of zopiclone at 9.30 p.m. On an empty stomach they would hit me like a train. Quite why I chose that time of night I'm not sure: I think it was the earliest I could take the dose without the effect wearing off before I went to bed.

A couple of hours before taking the pills, I would arrange them neatly on the coffee table. My friend Tim saw me do this once. 'You look like a hooker's client laying out his money in advance,' he said. But the analogy that occurs to me now is a religious one. It was like a parody of Holy Communion – including the fast that the faithful observe before receiving the sacrament. Once addiction fixes on things rather than people, rituals inevitably follow. Earlier I compared the rituals of the blackjack table to the rubrics of the Missal. Heroin users, too, treat knives, pipes and needles like sacred implements whose preparation is part of the high – which it probably is, since anticipation releases dopamine.

I don't know to what extent I was physically addicted to zopiclone: the glorious sensations of the first few months wore off quickly, while the nasty bits – the memory loss, the metallic taste in the mouth – lingered. My relationship with it was certainly unhealthy, but I didn't use it as a sleeping pill, because the quality of the sleep it produced was so poor. I'd wake up feeling dirty and exhausted. Other people who took zopiclone told me the same thing, so I thought GPs might eventually give up on it as an alternative to other sleeping pills.

Far from it: in 2007 nearly four and half million prescriptions for zopiclone were written in England. A report by Dr Russell Newcombe published in 2009 by the charity Lifeline revealed that 'zimmies' (from Zimovane) were a popular street drug in the north-east of England – sometimes in the form of 15 mg tablets not available in the UK, which suggests that they came from an internet pharmacy.[6]

One interviewee said heavy zopiclone users 'looked really evil', with their bloodshot eyes, messy hair, untidy clothes, drooling mouth and drunken sailor's gait. 'Trying to sit down can take them half an hour – it has to be seen to be believed, if it wasn't so sad it would be funny.' No wonder my friends gave me a wide berth. But those were the worst cases. For regular all-night partygoers, 'zimmies' were something to help you come down after a night on stimulants – the pattern Dr Max Pemberton described in the previous chapter.

DRUGSTORE COWBOYS

None of the young people I know in London take zopiclone for kicks – it would be a strange choice, given the available alternatives in a city this size. But several of them have been prescribed it as a sleeping pill. It turned out that my friends were using their parents' private doctors to sort out their sleeping problems, and that often the drug was prescribed in tandem with anti-depressants, which can't easily be abused recreationally.

What fascinates me is that young Britons from all backgrounds are now so familiar with the names and special effects of psychoactive medicines. 'I've been on escitalopram for depression since I split up with my boyfriend, with zopiclone if I can't sleep, though I prefer zolpidem because it's shorter-acting,' says Anna, 23.

Twenty years ago I felt like a freak because I knew the difference between Valium and Zimovane. Not any more.

●

Universities have their own problems with prescription drugs. 'Students ask me for modafinil all the time,' says a psychiatrist friend of mine who works at a university. His tone of voice is weary.

And does he give it to them?

'No. I don't like any of these drugs. Do we really know what effect they'll have on people's brains a few years down the line? Of course not – even if they've passed clinical tests, they're simply too new.'

Modafinil, manufactured by Cephalon, is a drug that boosts your memory even when you're sleep-deprived. It increases the levels of dopamine and serotonin in your brain, but doesn't generate the euphoric high associated with amphetamine drugs such as Adderall. According to a review of its properties in the journal *Neuropsychiatric Disease and Treatment*, 'its primary mechanism of action remains elusive'.[7] It's astonishing how often one reads those words, or something very similar, about a psychoactive drug that's already on the market. (As a footnote, it's interesting to learn from an article by Jonah Lehrer in *Wired* that two pharmaceutical giants, AstraZeneca and GlaxoSmithKline, have scaled back research into the brain because the effects of new drugs are simply too unpredictable in practice, however promising their formulations look on paper.)[8]

Modafinil isn't a cognitive enhancer in the sense that it makes you smarter. But it reduces the need for sleep and enables students to carry on studying while their peers are crashed out from exhaustion – so the distinction is a pretty fine one.

Here's a description of taking modafinil from a student interviewed by the York University newspaper, *Nouse*:

'In a typical modafinil-fuelled night, I take the drug with dinner, go to the pub with my friends and maybe watch a film, before getting in at around 1 a.m. and working for another eight hours. It's a productive way of living; it lets me be sociable and academic at the same time.'

What that really means, of course, is that he can dispense with the annoyingly time-consuming business of sleeping.

No one disputes that modafinil has an almost miraculous capacity to reduce the need for sleep: the US military has already approved it for use on Air Force missions. According to the *Scotsman*, the British Ministry of Defence 'has ploughed hundreds of thousands of pounds into researching whether they should follow the lead of forces including the French Foreign Legion and start using the drug to keep military personnel vigilant for up to 60 hours at a time.'[9]

The *Scotsman* refers disapprovingly to these 'secret pep pills', as if research on them were a scandalous misuse of public funds. But does Britain really want to find itself in a position where potential enemies are mentally more alert than its own personnel? Obviously not. Then again, what happens when you apply the same argument to competition between university students? Are they wrong to use psychoactive weapons to gain advantage over their peers?

Modafinil and Adderall are omnipresent on Ivy League campuses, where students imagine – with some justification, given how seriously Americans take education – that their entire futures rest on their Grade Point Average. They are also up against foreign students, especially from East Asia, with a well-earned reputation for phenomenally hard work (and less of an appetite for partying). So American kids are relying on these drugs to stop them slipping behind the competition.

One of the reasons American university students have slipped comfortably into prescription drug abuse is that so many of them spent their formative years taking Ritalin for ADD and ADHD. Of course, whether these maladies really exist is a controversial question. As we saw in the first part of this chapter, at least one leading American expert in the medication of children for attention deficit regards the diagnoses as questionable and the drug treatment as worse than useless.

But the statistics are clear: according to the US body Centers for Disease Control and Prevention, 'a million more kids had a parent-reported ADHD diagnosis in 2007 compared to 2003 – a 22 per cent increase'.[10]

Generally speaking, American and, increasingly, British schools don't have a problem with this sort of medication: perhaps the greatest beneficiaries of all are schoolteachers, for whom the effect of amphetamines on hyperactive students is nothing short of a disciplinary miracle. Universities are more anxious about it, however. They know that these drugs are being traded, and that – certainly in the case of Ritalin and Adderall – they can easily be recreationally abused by people whose 'attention deficit' is caused by partying all night.

According to Professor Sean Esteban McCabe at the University of Michigan's Substance Abuse Center, users of Adderall tend to be white male undergraduates at competitive universities. They are likely to be a member of a fraternity, have a GPA of 3.0 or below and regularly admit to taking other drugs. 'In other words, they are decent students at schools where, to be a great student, you have to give up a lot more partying than they're willing to give up.'[11]

By using Adderall, students are making the act of studying part of the overall hedonic experience of university: when poring over your books becomes pleasurable, the distinction between work and play is eroded. An article in the *New Yorker* in 2009 described the experiences of 'Alex', a Harvard student who used Adderall to reconstruct his weekly routine into a cycle of eating, drinking and studying, punctuated by long sleeps.

'When you conceive of what you have do to for school, it's not in terms of nine to five but in terms of what you can physically do in a week while still achieving a variety of goals in a variety of realms – social, romantic, sexual, extracurricular, résumé-building, academic commitments,' he said.

Alex mentioned a side effect of the drug I recognise from young friends with similar chemical enthusiasms. 'The number of times I've taken Adderall late at night and decided that, rather than starting my paper, hey, I'll organise my entire music library!'

Rebecca, the 25-year-old daughter of one of my friends, says that sounds very familiar: 'If an Adderall user drops from exhaustion, the culprit is as likely to be iTunes as a law textbook. At university, I used to live with a gay guy who became *obsessed* with making sure every album in his library was meticulously classified. Every Madonna track had the release date added, and every episode of *Buffy the Vampire Slayer* would have a concordance attached, along with the names of the directors and producers for every episode. It was astonishing. Like a work of art, really.

'I used to go to bed when he was "settling in" for the night. When I got up for a shower in the morning he'd still be there, eyes glued to the screen, feverishly re-entering metadata because he'd found "a better way to sort everything".'

Predictably, the consumption of brain-boosting drugs doesn't end with these students' final papers. Why stop using them when you're about to enter a work environment in which every week brings the sort of pressure you experienced before your final exams? The same *New Yorker* article described how cognitive-enhancing drugs are seeping into corporate life, quoting a reader who wrote to *Wired* complaining about 'a rising young star' who was 'using unprescribed modafinil to work crazy hours. Our boss has started getting on my case for not being as productive.'

It's hardly surprising that people don't think of these mind-altering drugs as a big deal when Cephalon describes Provigil, its brand name for modafinil, as a remedy for tiredness and 'decreased activity'. Hardly the 'excessive daytime sleepiness' mandated by its original government approval. The FDA reprimanded the company for this 'expansion' of labelling.[12]

Drugs such as modafinil and Adderall weren't a feature of British university life until recently. They made their first appearance at Oxford and Cambridge, from where they are slowly making their way down the university food chain.

I spoke to Lewis, 24, a recent graduate of one of Cambridge's grandest colleges. 'You've got to remember that Oxbridge undergraduates think they have more in common with the Ivy League than they do with students on redbrick campuses,' he said. 'Many of them learned about modafinil through talking to friends at Harvard and Yale on Facebook. And they thought, I want some of that, because I'm going to be entering the same sort of high-pressure environment as my Harvard buddies.'

He added: 'It's a sort of alpha male thing. An Ivy League wannabe would order shitloads of modafinil off the internet and sell it to friends who were planning to become corporate lawyers. What could be cooler than studying your arse off and not getting bored?'

What indeed? But let's go back to the article by L. Alan Sroufe quoted earlier. In addition to the damage these drugs may do to the people who take them, he says, they have another flaw: they don't actually deliver any long-term cognitive enhancement. Children's exam results pick up because they're concentrating, but the effect fades – leaving them with the withdrawal symptoms produced by taking psychostimulants for a long time.

Cambridge's alpha males may find that so-called cognitive-enhancing drugs improve their performance in Finals, but if they carry over their habit into a high-pressure workplace they could find themselves trapped by what once seemed to be a risk-free shortcut to success. As with the clubbers we described in the previous chapter, it might be worth checking on the state of their brain chemistry in a few years' time.

8
GAMING, THE
NEW GAMBLING

'Daddy, when are you coming to bed?'

In a basement office in Margate, Kent, a former lorry driver is clocking up his twelfth consecutive hour on the online role-playing game Second Life. Dennis, 48, runs his own haulage firm: a job that doesn't require much of his time but provides a comfortable income for his family. But the time he used to spend painting, reading and chatting to his wife is now entirely consumed by Second Life.

Most days, Dennis never gets dressed. He insists that meals be brought down to him in the basement according to a specific schedule, to coincide with arrangements for 'virtual meetings' that he has set up with other characters in the game. One of his daughters, four-year-old Katie, is used to hearing the sound of a bell ringing loudly from down below.

'Tea bell!' she says, cheerfully. When the drink is delivered, Dennis's eyes don't leave the screen. Occasionally he murmurs a weak thank you, but he barely notices food and drink arriving, and he often doesn't remember eating it.

In Second Life, Dennis plays nine distinct characters to obscure the fact that he plays so much. Each has an entire back story, and he has invented imaginary real-world 'owners' to go along with each of them. One character, Sabrina, is supposed to be 'Lesley' in real life: a 22-year-old student from Maidstone who chats, shops and deals in virtual real estate when she's not revising for her exams.

A key feature of Second Life is that, if you really know what you're doing, you can make quite a lot of (real) money by dealing in virtual property. Dennis estimates that he makes $2,000 a month from online real estate. These are modest sums by a serious virtual realtor's standards, but Dennis isn't there for the money.

Truth be told, he can't tell you why he is – only that, every morning, he wakes three hours before his wife and immediately goes downstairs, locks himself in his 'den', and loads the game. He admits that he likes the social element to it: he enjoys making up new personalities. And he also likes the way the game is designed to give what he calls 'regular feedback': a sense that his actions have big consequences.

'A few clicks, and castle shimmers into view, which I can decorate and start a family in,' he says. 'Provided I have enough Linden dollars.' Linden dollars are Second Life's currency, part of the complex set of reward systems engineered into the game. They are exchangeable for real money. Second Life players have made and lost US dollars as a result of speculating in 'virtual economics'.

Dennis is typical of the most compulsive class of Second Life user – the ones you see in forums explaining that their families are falling apart and that they can't hold down jobs. But he denies he is addicted to the game. 'Yeah, maybe I spend a bit too much time in front of the computer,' he says. 'But I'm not hurting anyone.'

What he doesn't tell me, but his wife does, is that last month she threatened to move out of the house, taking his two daughters with her.

•

'Sometimes I would love to throw my phone and computer out the window. Not because I'm frustrated with them, but because I feel that they are glued to me and drain me of all energy.'[1]

Ashley, writing on the Tokyo Housewife blog, is not the first American woman to become dependent on technology. While most obsessive internet users are male, academics are increasingly noting that women – especially those in their thirties and forties – are catching up fast.[2]

Where previously American housewives were addicted to gambling and to bidding wars on eBay, now they're becoming obsessed with simplistic games that have refined the reward dynamics of those two pastimes.

With eBay, users have to wait a week to receive whatever they've won. Gambling sites often trick players into spending too much money too quickly, which can cause trouble with husbands. But, while there's a limit to how much you can realistically spend within FarmVille, there seems no limit to the numbers of rewards and encouragements the game gives you to continue.

For the women who play these games, the 'virtual goods' they collect are just as real as their eBay purchases. 'These housewives are still spending money, but rather than having a garage full of junk they don't need, they're the proud owners of cattle and tractors on farm estates in Facebook,' says one technology journalist. 'Whether that's a step forward or a step back, I don't know.'

Are these women addicted to the internet? Do a Google search on 'internet addiction' and you'll find tests, self-help guides, articles about gamers dying from starvation, and thousands upon thousands of newspaper articles and pieces of academic research on the phenomenon.

A classic horror story surfaced in February 2012, when a Taiwanese man died while playing video games at an internet café in Taipei. Dozens of other patrons carried on for hours afterwards, apparently unaware that they were sitting near a corpse. Police said that a waitress found the 23-year-old sitting rigidly on a chair with his hands stretched out, and that he might have been dead for nine hours.[3] Despite his youth, however, he did have a history of heart problems and may have been killed by low temperatures. So he wasn't a victim of internet addiction, unless you choose to define it extremely loosely.

Most psychiatrists are suspicious of the term internet addiction, with good reason. In my opinion, it's best avoided: it's a bit like saying people are addicted to pubs rather than to alcohol. Logging on to the internet is like flicking between shopping channels, each dedicated to a different compulsion. Shouldn't we be blaming the underlying compulsions themselves rather than the technology that mediates them?

This isn't to deny that, for many people, it's getting harder and harder to drag themselves away from the internet. The addictive aura of these websites is becoming stronger – and it's undoubtedly the technology that's tightening the screws. Everyone knows that online gambling, gaming and pornography are addictive. It's less well known that their addictive potential is constantly being refined – dangerously so in the case of porn, as we'll see in the next chapter. Also, the lessons designers learn from experiments with gambling and porn are being applied to online pursuits that, on the face of it, seem too innocent and childlike to get people seriously hooked.

●

As the case of Dennis illustrates, it isn't just children who are getting trapped in cyberspace. Increasingly, we're taking our toys with us into adulthood. Like those fun cognitive-enhancing drugs, social technology is meddling with the boundaries between 'work' and 'play'. Where previously a service like Twitter, which is essentially a chat application like the MSN Messenger of the 1990s, would have been regarded as a social plaything, it's now part of the professional arsenal of communicative tools – sometimes even replacing email as a primary means of communication in the office.

GAMING, THE NEW GAMBLING

But Twitter is different from email in important ways. Like other 'web 2.0' products of the past decade, it is becoming increasingly 'gamified', as product companies pick up tips from gaming engineers about how to keep people hooked on their services. Your old email client was never designed to keep you in it for as long as possible, but Twitter is.

And consider Foursquare, an application that lets you 'check in' to real-world venues to let your friends know where you are at any given moment. (Mysteriously, the need to check in is felt most strongly by users when they are eating in a swanky restaurant or arriving in an exotic foreign city.) Foursquare awards 'badges' for various levels of accomplishments – 'achievements', they're called – using language and user interface elements that are plucked straight from a video game.

Applications developers look to social gaming companies such as Zynga in San Francisco for tips when building their products, because they know that the games its engineers create are among the most addictive experiences on the internet.

One of the ways developers such as Zynga keep people hooked is with 'design cues', elements of the user interface that signal some sort of reward. These get people excited and, like other addictive cues, generate dopamine.

In the case of Zynga's FarmVille, players receive visual hits every time they accomplish a task: for example, when they water or harvest a square of crops, they're treated to a short animation and cutesy sound effect. And as they watch the gold coins they've earned from growing and selling pile up in their virtual handbags, and are also rewarded for their actions with the pleasing 'whoosh' sound, they're encouraged to repeat those actions.

What's interesting is that such actions should be 'rewarded' at all. People who suffer from obsessive-compulsive disorders rarely derive any reward from them, but in this case meaningless, repetitive OCD-style actions are encouraged rather than frowned upon. It's not by accident that these pieces of software deluge the user with little fixes of social reinforcement and ego massage.

Significantly, these tricks are being picked up by non-gaming software companies. Modern applications are engineered to provide dozens of little hits per hour: the modern computer is becoming overloaded with intrusive notifications from Skype, Twitter, email, Facebook and any other software with a communication component. There's a piece of software for Macintosh computers called Growl that was specifically designed to streamline the various notifications. In practice, it's almost as invasive as the higgledy-piggledy world of individual notifications: it showers dozens of translucent rectangles across the screen every time a programme wants your attention. Infuriating, you might think. But the people who install Growl welcome the distraction. It makes them feel needed – and if the stream of notifications slows down they wonder why.

The user interfaces of applications that perform perfunctory office functions are beginning to resemble dashboards. Apple's OS X actually *has* a dashboard. The Dock, from which applications can be launched, has red status indicators – which are there to tell you, for example, that you have unread email. They are lifted directly from the video games of the late 1990s.

The result of this crafty borrowing is that people find it ever more difficult to drag themselves away from the screen. They admit as much, even if they don't use the word 'addicted'. But in terms of stickiness and brain-hijacking, every operating system pales in comparison with the latest video games.

●

Online gaming is the new gambling, and its growth in the last decade has been explosive. Gaming appears to be replacing online gambling as the addict's poison of choice. It does an even better job than virtual roulette wheels at hanging on to players.

Dennis used to gamble and drink excessively in his twenties and thirties. When he found himself with less disposable income in his early forties, these pursuits became less readily available. But business picked up again as he approached fifty – and so did his addictive behaviour. Presented with the choice of returning to drinking and the blackjack table or throwing himself into computer games, he chose a digital fix he could enjoy from his swivel chair.

Like many gaming addicts, Dennis was also lured in by the false impression that no money was changing hands in Second Life. He purchases Linden dollars with money from his PayPal account – but, as he says: 'It's like the foreign currency you spend on holiday. You don't think of it as real expenditure. At least, not until you check your fucking bank statements.'

The impetus for the switch from gambling to gaming was a law passed by the US government in 2006. After several failed attempts, Congress made online betting illegal and prevented any company from providing it to the US.[4] The reverberations were felt worldwide.

Jason Trost is an American who was forced to move to the UK in 2008 to establish his online betting company, Smarkets. He says: 'As it stands, many Americans engage in illegal online betting with offshore operators. But, obviously, the number of people gambling online in the US has been dramatically slashed since the law changed. These people are now looking for something else to do.

'Of course, with the big online US gambling providers getting shut down overnight, the global gambling scene became much more fragmented.'[5]

Game developers had been watching enviously for years as people got hooked on internet gambling. That's why so many former online gambling mechanics are now being recruited by gaming companies. These people aren't so much game programmers *or* gambling programmers: they're brain-hijackers with transferable skills, as one Silicon Valley gaming company CEO explained privately:

> We have a lot more flexibility than the old gambling sites did, in a way. They have to build experiences around real-world games like roulette and slot machines. We don't. We can make up whatever

we like, and toy with the mechanics behind the scenes to keep users engaged.

We design an environment in which losses are insignificant and there are regular reassurance mechanisms. Then we make modifications to that environment and monitor which combinations of punishment and encouragement keep users playing for longer. We engineer the game very precisely to keep players enjoying it for the longest possible time, and we use complex software to help us monitor what the entire installed user base of players is doing with their copy of the game.

We are learning what works by measuring it – we don't have to guess. That's what is so great about these new mobile social platforms – they offer us so much real-time data about the users.

In other words, as Rovio's Peter Vesterbacka said in the opening chapter, they just run the numbers.

Games don't only use rewards as a way of keeping players hooked: they also invent obstacles, or 'frustrations'. Carefully engineered frustrations exist in games of all complexities. For example, every so often a level is made significantly more difficult to complete than the last one. Often, the hurdle can be overcome by paying your way out of it – by purchasing a 'power pack', for example, via in-app purchasing. (Needless to say, purists look down their noses at these short-cuts.)

Even an apparently simple game like Angry Birds has little tricks up its sleeve to coax players out of a few more cents. Not everyone finds the game as easy to play as the whizzkids who get three stars on every level. For those who struggle, an in-app purchase called the Mighty Eagle is available. The Mighty Eagle will clear any level the player is struggling to complete. It costs $0.99 and can be reused infinitely.

'The thing about in-app purchases is that Apple has designed them to be as 'frictionless' as possible,' says the CEO quoted above, who was reluctant, like any app developer, to reveal too many ingredients of his secret sauce. 'You almost don't realise you've made a purchase with iOS [Apple's mobile operating system]. Once you've entered your email address, you can keep purchasing more virtual goods with a couple of clicks.

'It's a nightmare when children get hold of their parents' iPhones and start tapping away. Their parents inevitably come to us for refunds. That tells you something about how easy it is to keep spending money: two-year-olds can do it.'

Today's games offer a cornucopia of reward systems, each of them designed to toy with players' brains in a slightly different way. One of them is 'levelling up', an acknowledgement of social status within the game and the 21st-century version of an old-fashioned game score. The players who put in the most hours get the highest rewards: they are given the opportunity, for example, to purchase more advanced weaponry than their peers. Showing off about your 'level' is intoxicating. Players feel anxious about their place in the social hierarchy of the game and devote ever more time to raising their score.

GAMING, THE NEW GAMBLING

The games are carefully geared towards different categories of player. Boys are targeted with solitary but immersive fantasy universes, which are often better suited to consoles like the Xbox and PlayStation. If *Call of Duty* produces addiction in its players, it seems to be a characteristically male form of it.

But how do you addict women to gaming? Manufacturers have done a lot of research into this, and established that women enjoy social games that are played out in a context that includes contact with strangers and, often, a chat feature. FarmVille and Words with Friends are designed with these innate gender differences in mind. Housewives who spend most of their day looking after the home or their children often crave interactions with adults. Their boredom has a special quality that games manufacturers exploit ruthlessly.

A game designer who has worked for the BBC told me, off the record: 'It's well known in the industry that certain companies are quite deliberately making their products addictive. But it's something that isn't talked about very much, because it's hardly something to be proud of.'

What we're looking at here is the same clever opportunism displayed by coffee chains that force customers to pass by artfully arranged slices of carrot cake before they can order a cappuccino. The result in both cases is to create yet another social epidemic, born out of the marriage of marketing and reward-responsive brain chemistry. And yes, I know that using such language in these trivial contexts seems a bit pompous – but, make no mistake about it, that's what is going on.

THE FIX

In the words of one FarmVille addict: 'As I sit there, gazing at my pretty hedges and cherry trees, I feel like some lobotomised housewife from *Mad Men*.' Except, of course, she's far from lobotomised: with every minutely calculated purchase she makes for her farm, the chemicals in her brain produce a delicious little surge of gratification.

●

Ryan van Cleave is an American professor whose life was turned upside down by World of Warcraft (fans call it 'WoW'). He published a book about his experiences in 2010. Van Cleave wasn't as lucky as Dennis: his first chapter opens with an abortive suicide attempt he describes as the 'rock bottom' that jolted him into changing his habits. As van Cleave recounts his battle with WoW, he says things about gaming addiction which remind me of the obsessive behaviours we've examined in previous chapters. In fact, remove the computer and his confessionals could have come from the pages of any drug addict's or alcoholic's memoirs.[6] (Incidentally, van Cleave isn't in fact the professor's real name. He changed it in 2006 from Ryan G. Anderson. Van Cleave is the name of his World of Warcraft 'arena team'.)

Van Cleave, like Dennis, would often eat meals at the computer: 'microwave burritos, energy drinks, foods that required only one hand, leaving the other free to work the keyboard and mouse'.[7]

World of Warcraft made him feel positively godlike: 'I have ultimate control and can do what I want with few real repercussions. The real world makes me feel impotent ... a computer malfunction, a sobbing child, a suddenly dead cellphone battery – the littlest hitch in daily living feels profoundly disempowering.'

His academic career imploded thanks to his video game addiction. 'I took out a ton of student loans. That's how a gamer handles something: put things off until tomorrow.'

Van Cleave distinguishes between 'intrinsic' reward strategies, which include a player's position on the in-game 'hall of fame', and 'extrinsic' rewards – like the admiration of your friends after impressive in-game accomplishments. This is an arbitrary distinction. What matters is that we recognise the strategies of game developers who are intent on getting us ever more fixated on their products, their methods fortified by powerful data analysis tools and testing methods. These are made possible by new social platforms and pocket gaming systems like the iPhone. The point can't be stressed enough: people aren't getting addicted to these games by accident.

Game manufacturers love to tease players by offering them hints about the sorts of benefits they'll get at the next level. For example, in Z2Live's Battle Nations, the buildings you're able to buy are shown in colour, with gold 'prices' next to them. The ones you can't quite purchase yet are shown in grayscale. They feel tantalisingly close, but you can't have them until you've put in the hours, or dropped the cash, to level up.

Game developers layer their creations with different sorts of feedback mechanisms: World of Warcraft has 'quest rewards', 'talent points' and 'honour points' – each designed to tease and tickle the brain's reward systems in a slightly different way – while Battle Nations encourages users to collect resources to build cosmetic improvements to their military camps. You can see how these games flirt with self-esteem: a college drop-out in Connecticut with acne and coke-bottle spectacles can be a mighty warlord online.

'When you look at the time people waste on these games, you discover that the simpler ones aren't as dangerous, from the point of view of addiction,' says *Kernel* editor Milo Yiannopoulos. 'Angry Birds, for example, can be a mesmerising habit. But it's more of a time-waster than a home-wrecker.

'It's the large-scale games with the immersive fantasy universes that take over people's lives. That's partly because, like the famous Tetris game responsible for the Game Boy's success, they are unwinnable. Angry Birds can be completed – though there's always the option of going back and reworking old levels to get higher scores, and of course fiendishly tricky new spin-offs are released every few months. But there's no end to games like World of Warcraft.

'In other words, once it's got you sucked in, only a trigger from the real world – like a marriage breaking up, or a P45 landing on the door-mat – is likely to get you out again.'

●

As you might imagine, gaming is terrifically big business. To date, retail sales of just one franchise, *Call of Duty*, have topped $6 billion.[8] One game in the series, called *Black Ops*, raked in $650 million after being on sale for just five days. *Modern Warfare 2* took $550 million over the same period. Its sequel, *Modern Warfare 3*, took a staggering $400 million in Britain and the United States after just 24 hours on sale. It was the highest-grossing entertainment launch ever, dramatically overshadowing every Hollywood blockbuster.

Subscription games are just as lucrative. In November 2008, there were an estimated 11.5 million World of Warcraft subscribers worldwide.

Market researchers Forrester predict that computer gaming will soon overtake both recording and film as the number one entertainment industry by gross revenue. Zynga is currently valued at $6 billion, with over 220 million users. Eight million of them are paying players. And Zynga is just one company, which makes games primarily for the Facebook platform. Other developers, like EA and Blizzard, are raking in fortunes from other subscription models and the high cost of purchase of console games.

Though the costs of gaming are relatively small – subscriptions vary for the online fantasy games, but they're generally well under $100 a month, and even the flashiest new console games only have a list price of $60 or so – when users get hooked, as Dennis did, they often duplicate these amounts to maintain the parallel accounts required to sate their feverish appetites.

We've seen that the extraordinarily complicated reward mechanics engineered into modern games are designed, quite simply, to keep people playing for longer. Well, the tactics are working. So widespread

is the phenomenon of video game addiction and related online obsessions that an entire secondary industry is springing up all over the
world to cater specifically to those with addictions to gaming, texting,
surfing and even email. There are 300 internet addiction clinics in
China alone, catering to some of the estimated 17 million game and
internet addicts in that country.[9]

'They believe the virtual world is beautiful and fair,' says Dr Tao,
one of the doctors pressing for internet addiction to be classified as a
recognised mental disorder. 'In the real world, they become depressed,
upset, and restless – they are very unhappy.'

Tao says that as China's culture and society undergoes unsettling
transformations brought about by its rapid economic growth, its citizens are struggling to adapt. '[Internet addicts] can't adjust to school
and society, so they try to escape their difficulties and avoid problems.
They lack self-confidence and often don't have the courage to continue
their lives,' he says.

Jia Chunyang, a typical patient at the centre, stole money from his
parents and went on a 15-day gaming bender at a local net café while
his parents scoured the city looking for him. That was what landed him
in internet 'boot camp', as it's been called. Note the similarity between
his escapade and an alcoholic binge: the boy was physically as well as
psychologically lost for over two weeks, which is a long time for even
a bender to last.[10]

Such problems aren't restricted to the Far East. ReSTART,
in Fall City, Washington – appropriately, a suburb of computer-

obsessed Seattle – is one of America's first specialised digital addiction treatment centres. Its 45-day rehabilitation course, which treats those addicted to gaming, texting and the internet, costs $14,000.

Ben Alexander, a graduate of the course, told the Associated Press how his addiction began at university. 'At first, it was a couple of hours a day. By midway through the first semester, I was playing 16 or 17 hours a day.'

Alexander claims the treatment, which involves 'counselling and psychotherapy sessions, doing household chores, working on the centre's grounds, going on outings, exercising and baking cookies', was a success. 'I don't think I'll go back to World of Warcraft anytime soon,' he said.[11]

Even Angry Birds, which doesn't wreak anything like the same levels of havoc on people's lives, is responsible for some eyebrow-raising statistics. According to AYTM Market Research, 28 per cent of players reported feeling either 'always' or 'often' addicted to the game. Twelve per cent of people who have played it more than 25 times have deleted the app because they were worried it might eat up too much of their time. A further 12 per cent have considered a 'radical cure' for their habit.[12]

According to this research, 58 per cent of regular players reported an improvement in their mood when they fired up the game – clear evidence that Angry Birds is functioning as a portable and easily accessible quick fix for the millions of people who have installed the various editions of it on their mobile phones over 300 million times since it was released in December 2009.

●

It was inevitable, perhaps, that specialised websites should spring up to limit the damage caused by online gaming. One called wowdetox. com enables World of Warcraft addicts to share their stories about quitting the game, and just as often failing to. Enabled by the same technology that encouraged players to get addicted in the first place, it's a support group which provides a place for WoW players – and their 'WoW widows' – to share stories. There have been over 55,000 posts to date. Some make for reassuring reading:

> I started playing the evil known as WoW in December of 2008. 3 years later and countless numbers of hours logged into this game and i can finally say that I am WoW free. I just finished my first month of not playing this game at all. I actually logged on a few nights ago to send gold to people that i knew and had real life conversations with whiel playing, although i knew sending them gold wont help them quit, i still shared my sympathy with them about how i would like for them to consider quitting just like me. This game makes you a social reject and always keeps you coming back for more. Just like all the other testimonials on this site, they are almost all true. This game is so bad in so many ways. IT WILL RUIN YOUR LIFE IF YOU LET IT!!!! I actually just got married on

the 17th of december and honest to god, my gift to my wife was quitting this horribly addicting game. And let me tell you, the both of us have never been happier.[13]

But other messages are less encouraging, suggesting that for those who quit WoW, the next temptation is just around the corner: 'Done playing WoW, i've moved onto Star Wars the Old Republic!'[14] The messages reek of desperation, loneliness and helplessness.

Isolated teenagers often form the most significant relationships in their lives online. The consequences are often miserable. Former addicts point to the transitory nature of friendships born online: people become 'friends' too quickly, because in online role-playing games you need to be part of a crew to get the full experience. For example, in WoW you have to join a gang to participate in 'raids' on enemy stockpiles.

But these relationships end just as quickly. 'Friends' become another component in a player's virtual arsenal – an asset to be discarded when no longer useful. Friendships operate on an accelerated timescale. They become gamified.

Combine this ethos with the inbuilt volatility of social media interactions, and you end up with a generation of young gamers who have alarmingly ruthless approaches to 'friending' and 'deleting' other human beings – something that's a problem for users of social networks generally but is made worse by the competitive, impulsive ethos of the games themselves.

The most explicit video games create scenes of digital violence so extreme that they are closer to a serial killing rampage than even the bloodiest warfare. Some games even allow players to simulate an act of necrophilia on the body of a fallen opponent.

'Corpse-raping has become this cool joke among gamers,' explains Kevin, 24, himself a passionate gamer. 'The other day I saw my little brother get his character to squat on the face of a dead soldier and I was like, dude, what the fuck is going on? And he said, "Don't you know about corpse-raping?" – as if it was the most normal thing in the world.'

The raging passions aroused by video games have provoked an interesting and occasionally bad-tempered debate in the media. Digital utopians, who seem to think anything with an on-switch is intrinsically a good thing, scoff at warnings about gaming addiction. On the other side of the fence there are anti-gaming campaigners such as Baroness Greenfield, a professor of synaptic pharmacology at Oxford University who argues that digital technology is exacerbating autism spectrum disorders and leading to an increase in violence and distraction among children. *Guardian* columnist and author Ben Goldacre, a qualified psychiatrist, has criticised Greenfield for, among other things, failing to present her findings in a peer-reviewed academic paper. Nevertheless, the latest research would appear to support *some* of her concerns. A 2009 paper in *CyberPsychology and Behavior* highlights some of the real-world consequences of excessive gaming and social networking for young people. These include the compulsive need to check status updates and the negative effects on interpersonal relationships caused by Facebook-engendered jealousy and feuding.[15]

There's also the cross-pollinating effect of addictive urges to consider. In March 2010, the novelist and video game addict Tom Bissell wrote a powerful article for the *Observer* in which he described his struggles with cocaine and *Grand Theft Auto*.

His 'cross-addiction', as 12-step groups would describe it, began with a celebratory line of coke he shared with a friend the day he purchased a new instalment of the game. A toxic relationship between cocaine and videogaming soon established itself. He became unable to enjoy video games without getting high. 'I felt as intensely focused as a diamond-cutting laser,' he wrote of that defining moment. '*Grand Theft Auto* was ready to go.'[16]

Later, as his addiction took hold, Bissell began to feel powerless to resist the two obsessions.

> Soon I was sleeping in my clothes. Soon my hair was stiff and fragrantly unclean. Soon I was doing lines before my Estonian class, staying up for days, curating prodigious nosebleeds and spontaneously vomiting from exhaustion.
>
> Soon my pillowcases bore rusty coins of nasal drippage. Soon the only thing I could smell was something like the inside of an empty bottle of prescription medicine. Soon my bi-weekly phone call to my cocaine dealer was a weekly phone call.

Soon I was walking into the night, handing hundreds of dollars in cash to a Russian man whose name I did not even know, waiting in alleys for him to come back – which he always did, though I never fully expected him to – and retreating home, to my Xbox, to GTA IV, to the electrifying solitude of my mind at play in an anarchic digital world.

Soon I began to wonder why the only thing I seemed to like to do while on cocaine was play video games.

It would be interesting to know how many gamers are cross-addicted. A substantial number, I suspect, though the other addiction needn't be drugs. Ryan van Cleave was prone to overeating and other obsessive behaviours.

Perhaps even more troubling, though, are the ways in which new social technology is encouraging dramatically anti-social behaviour. Increasingly, the lives of people under 30 are being played out through social software and games. Social technology isn't just helping them to express themselves by providing convenient ways to self-publish online, or by providing a space to list their favourite books and recording artists. It is beginning to define who they are. As Facebook becomes ubiquitous, the worry is that relationships in the real world will resemble those in the digital one: transitory, accelerated, pragmatic associations that provide a hit of narcissistic reassurance rather than lasting bonds between close friends.

GAMING, THE NEW GAMBLING

Facebook's insistence on feeding 'nostalgia' to us in the form of old photos – say, of our partner with his ex-girlfriend, or a particularly injudicious update from two years ago – is forcing social media junkies to maintain, update and police their profiles as regularly as they water their crops in FarmVille.

The *Wall Street Journal* reported in January 2012 that puberty seems to be kicking in earlier and earlier for young people. 'What teenagers want most of all are social rewards,' wrote Alison Gopnik.[17] It isn't obscenely fanciful to suppose that endless social reinforcement from new media and over-rewarding video games are having an effect on human development.

Does all this sound far-fetched? Consider one last statistic: by the end of 2011, Facebook was being cited in *a third* of divorce cases in the UK.[18]

9

REDISCOVERING
PORN

Of all the subjects people are likely to lie to researchers about, masturbating in front of a computer must be very near the top of the list. As a result, one of the fastest spreading addictions in the world today is also one of the least researched and least discussed.

That suits most of us. People generally don't want 'too much information' on this topic. Yet what information we do have suggests that the sexual appetites of countless millions of people are being manipulated in ways for which there is no historical precedent.

If that sounds melodramatic, consider the statistics. Since 2006 there has been an explosion of free porn on the internet, as X-rated rivals to YouTube such as Xtube have swept away the old pay-per-view model. Newspaper articles often claim that porn sites attract 72 million unique users every month – but that figure is based on research from before the free porn revolution. The numbers of hits on Xtube suggest that it's a gross underestimate.

REDISCOVERING PORN

The videos uploaded to the site by one gay couple from Boston calling themselves the Maverick Men had been viewed 90 million times by 2011. Manwin, the Montreal-based company that owns Xtube and many hard-core and fetish websites, attracts 42 million unique users to its tube sites alone *every day*.[1] The number of people who visit porn sites in a year probably exceeds 150 million – more than the population of Britain and France combined. As the developing world hooks up to the internet, that total will rise to hundreds of millions.

Of these, how many will develop an addiction? We can't be sure, not least because – as usual – there is no simple way of defining addiction. Another often-quoted statistic is that 10 per cent of American adults confess to having used porn 'addictively', which is a more sensible way to put it. What is undeniable is that habitual use of pornography on this scale was unknown before the advent of the World Wide Web, and for a good reason: the internet has an almost magical ability to arouse male sexual cravings.

The numbers tell only part of the story, however, and not necessarily the most important part. It's not just that digital technology creates unprecedented desire for pornography: the images themselves are shockingly explicit compared to most pre-digital porn.

Never before have so many nice people discovered that they have depraved sexual tastes. Husbands who would once have retreated to their dens to pore over car magazines now download videos of 'teen sluts' dressed as schoolgirls being violently fucked and gasping for more. These are men who thought they had grown out of pornography and, even now, would consider it undignified to buy a 'dirty mag'.

The difference between old-fashioned porn and internet porn is like the difference between wine and spirits. After hundreds of years as a mild intoxicant, pornography has undergone a crude distillation. Digital porn is the equivalent of cheap gin in Georgian England: it provides a reliable, dirty hit that relieves misery and boredom. You don't know how strong it is until you've tried it – at which point you may discover, too late, that you're wrestling with obsessions that until a few years ago you thought were confined to ferret-faced men in raincoats hanging around school playgrounds.

Internet porn has the same power as many addictive substances to rewire the brain's reward circuits. Only a minority of users are severely affected, but let's not forget that we're talking about a minority of 150 million people and rising. You don't have to believe that addiction is a 'disease' to recognise that this is one of the fastest-growing compulsions since the spread of cigarette smoking a century ago. Of all the addictions described in this book, it's the one that comes closest to panicking the experts.

Two things distinguish internet porn from traditional pornography. The first is the increasing sophistication of the technology that delivers porn, which makes it available on platforms and in places where it never was before – your son's iPad, for example. The second is the shift from soft-core to hard-core material.

No one believes that these are unconnected. The explosion of technological possibilities is pushing people's tastes towards explicit, bizarre, cruel and macabre images. But why should this be? How much of the blame lies with cynical porn manufacturers using extreme material to restore jaded appetites? How much of the change is the result of the unforeseen collision of sexuality and technology? Above all, what does internet porn *do* to the brains of millions of people so that their sexual preferences become so painfully warped?

●

'I used to have to go out of my way, to special stores. Now you'd have to be a clam shell on the moon to avoid it.' That's the voice of a 65-year-old American man who is struggling to control his addiction to pornography. He sounds astonished by the way the floodgates of porn have suddenly opened as he reaches retirement age (though presumably, since he's an addict, he must have welcomed it at first).

'The way people access porn has changed drastically since I was a teenager.' That is Robert, aged only 24. He's a graduate of London University who recently started his first job in publishing. 'When I first arrived at an all-boys boarding school in 2000, the security staff would search for porn magazines just as they would search for other contraband like cigarettes, pot or cheap vodka. But by the time I did my A-levels, most of the pupils had personal laptops. The boys became experts at hiding videos and images in obscure parts of their hard drives – so even the school's IT department couldn't catch them.

'The process was simple: you would source a DVD from a Hong Kong Chinese "porn king" – every year seemed to have one – and then, even if you passed it on to someone else, they could upload the content on to their laptop and destroy the hard evidence. Around that time, porn also became portable, so it wouldn't be uncommon for someone in sixth form to have a few videos saved on their smartphone or iPod – and to secretly pass their devices around the classroom.'

Whether you're 65 or 24, the social significance of pornography has changed drastically since you were an adolescent. The older man will have seen it grow steadily during the 1970s and 80s. First *Playboy* and *Penthouse* pushed their way into an increasingly eroticised popular culture; then VHS videos and cable television channels made it possible to watch porn movies in private. But it wasn't until the mid 1990s, when pornography went online, that it became easy to binge on self-renewing supplies of erotica.

Robert, in contrast, arrived at school at a time when there were already millions of porn images on the internet; the difficulty was gaining access to them. By the time he left, that problem had been solved. The school didn't relax its standards. It was outsmarted by technology – and by pupils who understand it better than the school authorities. They are getting more tech-savvy by the year.

'Since I left, the school has set up an internet network so the boys can get online in their rooms,' he says. 'There are parental locks and other safeguards, but a resourceful 13-year-old could get round most of them. And now that most of the kids have got iPads as well, sharing high-definition videos has never been easier.'

I was interested by a story Robert told me about the boy in his year who preferred porn magazines to online videos. He would visit a newsagent near the school to buy them – and was regarded as 'a bit of pervert' for doing so. Yet the content of these magazines was far less perverted than the smartphone videos of women being gang-banged that were passed around with a snigger underneath the desks.

None of these boys was old enough to remember the days when buying a top-shelf magazine was a rite of passage for teenagers. But what lingered in the tribal memory was the fact that 'wank mags' were popular with sad old men. Footage of violent sex was regarded as less contaminating than an artfully posed centrefold because the platform, the latest mobile phone or iPod, was cooler than a tacky magazine.

There was absolutely nothing cool about porn for my generation of schoolboys, born in the 1960s. Buying the stuff induced sweaty anxiety in the (invariably male) customer, and probably had done for centuries. You can sense it when you read Samuel Pepys's reference to buying 'an idle roguish book … in plain binding' which he resolved to destroy as soon as he had finished with it.[2] I wasn't brave enough to buy porn magazines, which isn't to say I never 'read' other people's. But I do remember watching people furtively snatching a magazine from the top shelf of the newsagents.

In fact, I remember it every week, when I buy my cappuccino in the self-consciously chic, mock-Italian coffee bar near my flat in

Notting Hill. Twenty-five years ago, the café was a grimy little corner shop where sex-starved van drivers and lonely pensioners stocked up on porn. These days the top shelf has been replaced by a rack for the European newspapers read by the young French and German bankers who hang out there on a Saturday morning with their girlfriends. But the irony is that – thanks to technology – these men have probably consumed far more pornography than the original shame-faced customers in the 1980s.

There is, after all, just so much more of it about. In 2006 (the last year for which detailed statistics were compiled) 4.2 million websites contained pornography: that is 12 per cent of all websites. There were 1.5 billion pornographic downloads every month, amounting to 35 per cent of all downloads. The only transaction necessary involved a credit card – risky, but not humiliating. And since the arrival of free tube videos it has been easy to develop an intense porn habit without spending a cent.

No one predicted that porn would be quite so pervasive in the early 21st century. But even if an earlier generation had foreseen this flood of computer pornography, I don't think anyone would have anticipated the features of porn that unnerve us most today: the massive appeal of hard-core images, often involving teenagers or children; and its transformation from a bad habit into an addiction.

•

When I was a young man I never saw the 'hard porn' written about in the newspapers. Some of the grainy VHS videos I watched were crudely explicit, but they didn't involve violence, fetishes or underage models. People who were into that sort of thing were thought of as sinister or psychologically unhinged. Not only did they have inexplicable tastes, but in order to indulge them they had to take risks. The more specialised the impulses, the greater the risk. S&M pornography involved visits to sex shops or panic-inducing deliveries by post – unless you joined the leather scene, in which case finding erotic material was easy but you were forced to live a double life. As for paedophiles, they behaved like secret agents, passing photographs to each other as if they were classified documents.

Not any longer. There are an estimated 100,000 websites on the internet containing illegal images. The most disgusting pictures, involving assaults on small children, are hidden away from search engines in the so-called deep web, uncharted cyberspace that requires special Freenet software to enter. More than two million people have downloaded this software; we don't know how many use it to view illegal porn, since recent upgrades hide not only the identities of users but also the fact that they're using Freenet in the first place.[3]

It's creepy to imagine paedophiles crawling through the deep web like strange creatures at the bottom of the ocean. The temptation is to write them off as freaks operating in a remote corner of the internet that we'd never visit ourselves. It's the job of the police to catch them.

But what are the police supposed to about the rising number of porn users who like their 'sluts' to be 'barely legal'? There were 14 million internet searches for 'teen sex' in 2006. Most of these will have led to porn sites whose owners claim that all their models are over 18. That may or may not be true. The important thing is that the models *look* as if they're below the age of consent.

One of the growth areas in porn is PCP, pseudo-child pornography. These websites employ what Sharna Olfman, a professor of psychology at Point Park University, Pittsburgh, calls 'childified women'. The models may be over 18, but they have adolescent faces. With the help of make-up, props and digital special effects, they can be made to look like children. 'It is not unusual to see a female porn performer wearing a school uniform, sucking a lollipop, and hugging a teddy bear as she masturbates with a dildo,' she writes.[4]

Despite its supposedly jokey overtones, PCP is pulling consumers in the direction of underage pornography. Countless other websites do the same. Many of the most popular gay porn sites, for example, contain galleries of boys who look more like 16 than 18; they're younger-looking than the mullet-haired teenagers who featured in the gay magazines of the 1980s. But age is not the only boundary that is shifting. There's also a drift towards violence and cruelty.

'Images today have become so extreme that what used to be hardcore is now mainstream pornography,' says Gail Dines, a sociology professor who is America's best-known authority on the effect of porn on women. 'Rather than sporadic trips into a world of coy smiles, provocative poses and glimpses of semi-shaved female genitalia, youth today are catapulted into a world of ravaged anuses, distended vaginas and semen-smeared faces.'[5]

And, as she points out, this isn't special kinky porn hidden in the deep web or behind a pay-wall: these are the free images you see if you log on casually to an adult website. Much of this material comes under the heading of 'gonzo porn', no-frills videos that dispense with those comically unconvincing storylines involving lonely middle-class housewives and oversexed plumbers. Instead, the viewer is plunged into hard-core action complete with writhing, gasping and close-up shots of genitalia.

How do we account for this across-the-board brutalisation of taste – this shifting of the centre of gravity from soft to hard porn?

●

In the past, every time a new medium of communication was invented, pornography jumped right in. Printing, photography, cinema, cable TV – they were all instantly spewing out porn. Bizarrely, the other genre that's good at riding these technological waves is Bible prophecy: printing presses, independent TV stations and online ministries were churning out apocalyptic material long before mainstream religion exploited the new media. As a communications professor put it to me just as the internet was taking off: 'It's the old mixture – prophecy and porn.'

Actually, pornography has not merely been exploiting the latest means of communication. It's been helping to create them. 'Premium cable' was developed to meet the needs of the adult entertainment market. Hotel chains invested heavily in pay-per-view channels. One reason VHS video triumphed over Betamax was that VHS was the format of choice for porn home rentals. Later, porn helped popularise CD-ROMs and DVDs.

Two things were happening simultaneously. Porn studios diversified their products, testing a rapidly growing market with more explicit movies. At the same time, different types of porn converged on to a single platform. You could move along the X-rated spectrum by flicking to a different channel or switching from TV to VCR.

So it would be wrong to think of the wild over-stimulation of the sexual imagination by the internet as arriving out of nowhere. That said, much of the technology on the internet was designed to lure people into watching porn. The development of broadband owed a lot to pressure from the adult entertainment industry, which also pioneered micropayments and user-uploaded videos. Coders working for porn sites taught the rest of the industry how to manipulate viewers by bombarding them with bewildering choices. The network of links joining porn galleries to videos and webcams is so intricate that porn surfers can lose track of where they are on the soft- to hard-core spectrum.

This confusion is deliberately engineered. One technical trick is to redirect viewers to explicit material that they hadn't intended to see, tempting them from free to commercial websites. In an article for *New York* magazine in 2011, Benjamin Wallace described what it's like to enter an increasingly dense porn jungle:

REDISCOVERING PORN

There you are, Porn Surfer, Googling your way to a little adult material – you know, a little plain-vanilla, middle-of-the-road, grown-up content – when, wham you've dropped acid and been astrally projected into a triple-X pachinko parlour ... You're in free-fall through this insane, cross-linking wilderness-of-mirrors chaos of pop-ups and pop-unders and portals and paysites. And, wait, why is someone called Jasmin talking to you in that browser window that just opened, as if you'd accidentally paid for a live cam show? ... You start to nurse a deep suspicion that there's more going on here than you can see – that there is some intricate, invisible web of revenue-sharing and traffic-trading and content licensing at work. Which, of course, there is.[6]

Many of the most powerful corporations in the world make money from pornography. Some have no choice but to be open about it, as in the case of porn distributor Time Warner Cable. Some, as in the case of Microsoft, are sheepish about the profits they make from pornographers buying their software. Often, companies hide their connections to the porn industry in 'opaque financial statements, SEC filings, and corporate red tape', to quote tech writer Blake Robinson.[7]

As in the world of tech generally, innovators are pushing aside big corporations. Tube sites are disrupting the business models of companies that, until very recently, were banking on a dominant market share of an ever-growing pool of paying customers. Now, there's big money to be made in businesses that provide distribution for free, home-made videos. These companies create websites, license movies from the traditional porn publishers and host amateur video. They don't make their own content, so their margins are much higher than those of the adult studios.

Gail Dines thinks the free market explains the drift towards hard-core porn. The low cost of entry and the intense competition to find and hold users have opened up extreme possibilities, she says. 'It is perhaps not surprising that Web-based competition for eyes and wallets is fuelling a rapid increase in porn depicting extreme situations, violence and pseudo-child pornography.'[8]

What she's suggesting is that sudden technological changes in an unregulated market are bound to produce a 'pushing of the envelope'. We've seen it happen in the entertainment industry often enough. As choice expands, consumers get bored and the producers try to hold on to their attention with more shocking material. Think of the way horror movies became increasingly blood-drenched between the 1960s and the 1990s. But even the most violent video nasties didn't trigger a compulsive reaction in ordinary viewers. Although *Driller Killer* and *Cannibal Holocaust* provided a cheap thrill for students, they didn't hijack the leisure time of vast numbers of middle-aged men secretly addicted to gore-fests. Nor did the leap from television screen to computer monitor intensify people's relationship with horror films. It's true that you can watch atrocities on the internet that you couldn't find in video stores. But, for most people, seeing this stuff once is more than enough: it's a niche market for disturbed loners.

REDISCOVERING PORN

Pornography is different. The online audience exhibits an interesting mixture of reactions. It's easily aroused to a state of craving – but easily bored. That combination is typical of addiction. Although the appetite for pornography seems insatiable, this is a volatile market. It's super-sensitive to new stimulants, for reasons that are as much biological as technological. Right from the beginning, internet porn has displayed a powerful capacity to interfere with the chemistry of the brain.

•

Internet porn arouses deep fears, especially among parents. The public is looking for simple answers – and simple solutions. In America, especially, the science has political overtones. Empirical claims about porn addiction have been turned into ammunition by participants in the culture wars.

In November 2004, the US Senate held a committee hearing on 'The Science of Pornography Addiction'. Dr Judith Reisman, a prominent crusader against pornography, told the committee: 'We now know that pornographic visual images imprint and alter the brain, triggering an instant, involuntary, but lasting, biochemical memory trail, arguably subverting the First Amendment by overriding the cognitive speech process. This is true of so-called 'soft-core' and 'hard-core' pornography. And once new neurochemical pathways are established they are difficult or impossible to delete.'[9] Reisman even produced a new name for chemicals released by porn: 'eroto-toxins'.

This sounded terrifying. But other academics tore apart Reisman's theories. Dr Daniel Linz, a psychologist at the University of California Santa Barbara, dismissed the concept of eroto-toxins as fiction. There was no evidence that porn left a special 'biochemical memory trail' that could not be erased. Internet porn addiction, like sex addiction in general, was probably learned behaviour that could be un-learned.[10] *Wired* magazine agreed, reporting the hearings under the tongue-in-cheek headline: 'Internet Porn – Worse Than Crack?'[11]

In the years since 2004, the flourishing of internet porn has undermined both sides in this debate. No one has demonstrated the existence of eroto-toxins, and the idea that they rob us of the power of free speech belongs in the 'reefer madness' category of scaremongering. On the other hand, the volume of internet porn has roughly doubled since the Senate hearings.

If this is learned behaviour, then tens of millions of people have recently picked up this knowledge, and they aren't finding it easy to un-learn. Therapists have found that weaning a porn addict off erotic websites can be as challenging as persuading an alcoholic to stay sober. Recovering porn users go through withdrawal symptoms. And the magnetic attraction of extreme porn is stronger than ever.

In his book *The Brain that Changes Itself*, referred to in Chapter 3, the psychiatrist Norman Doidge highlights the distinction between dopamine-driven 'wanting' and endorphin-driven 'liking'. (Doidge calls them 'exciting' and 'satisfying' pleasure, which amounts to the same thing.)[12] As we've seen, dopamine levels rise when drug addicts are presented with cues. I recently heard a former cocaine addict tell a Narcotics Anonymous meeting: 'The real hit isn't snorting the drug – it's hearing your dealer telling you he's got some for you.' Compulsive porn users know that feeling, too. Finding the right image can be more exciting than masturbating to it.

Doidge is convinced that internet porn is addictive in roughly the same way as drugs. Repeated, sudden releases of dopamine mean that 'wanting' becomes easy to switch on but hard to satisfy with 'liking'.

Doidge first noticed this happening to male patients of his in the mid to late 1990s, when porn started colonising the internet. 'Each had acquired a taste for a kind of pornography that, to a greater or lesser extent, troubled or even disgusted him, had a disturbing effect on the pattern of his sexual excitement and ultimately affected his relationships and sexual potency,' he says. What was happening to them? Pornography offers 'an endless harem of sexual objects,' says Doidge. This harem analogy is a familiar one in studies of porn and it's particularly appropriate to internet porn, in which so many sexual models are on offer simultaneously.

This degree of choice is something that appeals to men more than to women. Males right across the animal kingdom have evolved to seek sexual novelty; they are not naturally monogamous. This applies as much to gay men as it does to straight men. So one of the reasons a porn website is more potent than a dirty magazine is that it taps more directly into male evolutionary urges.

Moreover, dopamine is highly responsive to novelty, and digital technology is all about creating novel images. This sense of being spoilt for choice hyperactivates the appetitive system, explains Doidge.

'Porn viewers develop new maps in their brains, based on the photos and videos they see. Because it is a use-it-or-lose-it brain, when we develop a map area, we long to keep it activated. Just as our muscles become impatient for exercise if we've been sitting all day, so do our senses hunger to be stimulated.' The longer his patients spent at their computers, the more firmly porn images became wired into the pleasure centres of their brains. Also, 'the content of what they found exciting changed as the websites introduced themes and scripts that altered their brains without their awareness'.

This may sound a bit like Judith Reisman's eroto-toxins theory. Actually, it's a good deal more complicated. Doidge is a specialist in the brain's neuroplasticity – its ability to change its anatomy with thoughts and acts that turn genes on and off. It's a competitive process in which the brain appropriates new images at the expense of what had previously excited it.

Does internet porn simply reveal kinky tastes or does it also help create them? Dr Heather Wood of the Portman Clinic in London, which treats paedophiles and other sex offenders, told me: 'It's definitely a mistake to think that the internet creates ideas – it fans the flames of ideas that are already there in some form.'[13] Most therapists think that online fantasies bear some relationship to childhood experiences. Norman Doidge employs a Freudian model: porn latches on to aspects of sexuality created unconsciously during infancy. So, for example, boys who in early childhood feel dominated by their mothers may develop a 'residual unconscious female identification' that is unmasked by lesbian porn.

Like most Freudian hypotheses, this is difficult to prove and requires a leap of the imagination – but Doidge's explanation for how internet porn 'wires together' repressed elements in sexuality is a compelling one.

'Porn sites generate catalogues of common kinks and mix them together in images,' he writes. 'Sooner or later the surfer finds a killer combination that presses a number of his sexual buttons at once. Then he reinforces the network by viewing the images repeatedly, masturbating, releasing dopamine and strengthening these networks … Because he often develops tolerance, the pleasure of sexual discharge must be supplemented with the pleasure of an aggressive release, and sexual and aggressive images are increasingly mingled – hence the increase in sadomasochistic themes in hard-core porn.'

●

While I was researching this chapter I was introduced to a man I'll call Paul, who works for a well-known law firm in New York City. He was in his thirties, short, balding, chubby and with an off-putting habit of wringing his hands every time he was asked a question. He had grown up in a devoutly Jewish household on Long Island and was a virgin when he met his long-term girlfriend at the age of 27. This I know because Paul didn't seem to recognise such a thing as a conversational boundary and was happy to share intimate details of his sex life with virtual strangers.

Anyway, Paul had split up with his girlfriend a year earlier. He didn't have the self-confidence to seek out a new partner and had no interest in hookers. Instead, he became addicted to crack cocaine. This is something that can happen surprisingly easily to high-earning New Yorkers. The drug has long since moved out of the black ghettos. In his memoir *Portrait of an Addict as a Young Man*, literary agent Bill Clegg describes how he became hopelessly addicted to crack after a respected lawyer asked him if he'd ever freebased, and he lied and said yes and took a suck on the pipe.[14] Paul had a similar experience; a divorced woman he was hoping to date produced a crack pipe and he accepted out of bravado.

The two had sex. 'On one level it wasn't great,' Paul told me, 'but on another it was out of this world, because it produced the most mind-blowingly intense orgasm of my life. I already knew regular cocaine made you horny, but crack? That was something else.'

Paul found himself driving into dangerous neighbourhoods of the city in order to buy crack. 'It's amazing I wasn't robbed or killed,' he says. 'If anything, the dealers seemed amused to find that fat little Jewish guy in a business suit begging them for a fix – though no doubt I got ripped off pretty badly.'

Back home in his Brooklyn brownstone, Paul smoked crack every night and soon found the intensity of the mental hit wearing off. 'But the arousal and the orgasms didn't. And because I didn't have a girl-friend, I got very, very heavily into internet porn in order to take full advantage of the situation.

'I could stay in the same state of delicious anticipation for hours – days – at a time. I set up two monitors so I didn't miss what was happening on different sites. And I bought a vibrator. Actually, two vibrators. Internet porn took over my life, ruined my friendships and endangered my career – but of course I *had* to have crack to make it work for me. In the end, I went into rehab for crack, and that was the end of internet porn for me. My libido was gone.'

●

Internet porn takes apparently ordinary people to dark places that they thought were beyond their imagination. I realised this when, within a relatively short space of time, not one but two Catholic parish priests in Reading, the Thames Valley town where I grew up, were convicted of downloading child porn.

The reaction of the local community was one of disbelief. That may seem naïve, given the paedophile priest scandals engulfing the Roman Catholic Church – but I was taken aback, too, despite having reported on American clergy scandals for the *Daily Telegraph*.

One of the priests was the dean of Reading's Catholic clergy. I'd heard that he was hugely popular and likely to be promoted, but I'd never met him. The other priest I did know slightly because I'd attended a few of his Masses. He had the bustling, wafer-thin joviality typical of an overworked clergyman. His sermons were bland and wholesome. It was hard to imagine him becoming addicted to anything stronger than boiled sweets.

Records of the court cases leave us in no doubt that both priests were, as their defence lawyers insisted, truly addicted to porn. Both downloaded images of children. The headlines in the local papers didn't imply a moral distinction between them.

But there was one – though this is a difficult point to make in a society in which all child porn offences are considered to be equivalent to paedophile assault. One priest indulged in monstrous fantasies. The other seems to have crossed the line from legal to illegal images by accident. Moreover, a comparison of the two cases suggests that porn can drive people to commit apparently similar offences in quite different ways.

The first priest to be caught was Fr Michael O'Kelly, 47, local dean and parish priest of English Martyrs, a red-brick Italianate church familiar to me from my schooldays.

On 21 October 2001, worshippers arrived at Mass to be greeted by the Rt Rev Crispian Hollis, Bishop of Portsmouth. In the modern Catholic Church, it's a sign of the times that if the remote figure of a diocesan bishop unexpectedly materialises at a parish church, there's a good chance that there have been sex allegations against the priest. Fr O'Kelly had been arrested two days earlier. Bishop Hollis was as gentle as possible: 'Father Michael is well. He's okay and beginning the process of coming to terms with what has happened.'

But what the bishop couldn't conceal – it had already been in the media – was that police had seized child pornography from the presbytery. 'It is a vile trade. Woe betide anyone involved in it,' he said. O'Kelly's case reached court in March 2002, when he confessed to downloading material that the local newspaper said was too disgusting to describe in detail. 'It ranged from children to "babes in arms", and there were also some pictures of bestiality. Magistrates were shown a selection of the images in their private room, but they had to have a police "escort" or they would have been technically committing a crime themselves.'

In the witness box, O'Kelly was quick to blame the internet. 'It ignited a fascination which I had not been aware of,' he said. 'It became a habit, not a question of looking at the top shelf in a shop but items in the privacy of my own room. Japanese sites sparked a fascination of children. The images were horrible but I could not control it ... I allowed myself to follow links here and there. I was afraid but I followed.'[15]

Whether O'Kelly was really afraid or just making excuses is open to question – but his defence solicitor made one comment that does shed light on his actions. The priest, he said, 'acted like a collector, storing the images rather than poring over them for hours'. That seems to be true. O'Kelly, later sentenced to nine months in prison, downloaded an astonishing 30,000 photographs on to his computer, many of which were duplicates. He couldn't have looked closely at more than a small percentage.

The photographs showing children being raped are no less disgusting because they were filed away rather than opened – but that word 'collector' is interesting in the context of supposed compulsion. When I read it, I remembered a conversation I had with Dr April Benson, a New York therapist who treats shopping addiction: she said that some men use the notion of 'collecting' things to disguise what is actually a type of addiction. Indeed, hoarding is a familiar symptom of obsessive-compulsive disorder, otherwise known as OCD.

In the popular imagination, OCD is associated with the repetitive washing of hands, or constantly returning to the house to make sure the gas is turned off. In fact, the disorder encompasses a vast repertoire of rituals in which actions are performed in special sequences and objects arranged in special patterns in order to stave off anxiety.

Internet pornography can unearth obsessive-compulsive traits. Enter the words 'collector jailed' into a search engine, and you immediately come across stories about the compulsive hoarding of internet porn. An accounts clerk from Lincolnshire was jailed for downloading the largest collection of child pornography discovered in the UK – 500,000 images. In Pittsburgh, a man was jailed after police found 60 hard drives filled with images of underage girls; the defence tried to claim that Tourette's syndrome had led him to collect them compulsively. In any case hoarding on this scale would have been impossible without access to internet porn. The same goes for the O'Kelly scandal. These cases came to light because the material was illegal – but we should also bear in mind that the same technology allows men to amass large collections of images that may be explicit but don't actually break the law.

It's hard to see, in fact, how anyone with an obsessive-compulsive personality *and* a weakness for online porn can avoid getting the two mixed up. The internet enables users to painlessly download and catalogue thousands of files; arranging them is often part of the fun of owning a personal computer. Add sex to the experience, and collecting porn can turn into an all-consuming pastime.

Dean, a 45-year-old American lab technician, told me: 'I've been pretty much hooked on internet porn for five years, and every year I spend longer in front of my laptop. But the actual jerking off? I reckon I do less of that because arranging the pictures takes so damn long. Every software upgrade persuades me to start over, to refresh my palate. But the searching! It swallows up time in a way that the TV doesn't. I log on for half an hour before midnight and when I look at the clock it's three in the morning. It's like telling yourself you'll only pour one glass from the bottle. And it is a bit like being drunk, because time is speeded up. Or it can feel like being chained to a slot machine.'

In his everyday life, Dean doesn't show symptoms of OCD – but his incessant shuffling of photos and videos into folders sounds like obsessive-compulsive behaviour. Also, that reference to a slot machine is revealing. Slot machines offer rewards according to 'variable ratio reinforcement', in which gamblers are hooked by the randomness of the results. When Dean clicks his way through hundreds of thumbnail photos of women with shaved vaginas – his personal turn-on – he doesn't know whether the next one will arouse him (nor does the website owner, of course). One picture in 20, say, is arousing enough to save, but they're unevenly distributed around the galleries, so he keeps clicking until he's exhausted. 'I get fussier as time goes on – the image has to be just right, so I end up passing over pictures that would've really excited me a couple of years ago.'

This creeping fussiness is typical of today's porn users. We're talking about more than a simple slot-machine mechanism: a better analogy might be with a computer game. Lots of games do, in fact, make use of variable ratio reinforcement, but with extra features that manipulate the level of tension – for example, by plunging users into mini-cliffhangers at ever-shorter intervals. As we saw in the previous chapter, the excitement is gradually cranked up, as gamers break through to new levels of experience. Each is more intense than the last, but there is also a momentary release of tension.

Does some internet porn achieve a similar effect? I think it can do, and that this goes some way to explaining the drift towards extreme images.

An unhappily married man who takes up porn surfing knowing vaguely that he's attracted to younger women may end up trapped in the rough equivalent of a computer game. Every time he clicks on a link that's riskier than the previous one, he breaks through to a new level of experience. Before long he has crossed the border into images of pubescent girls.

This isn't to say that he's following carefully planned cues: the messy world of online porn doesn't work so systematically. But gamers and porn surfers who push themselves to physically exhausting extremes may be responding to similar obsessive-compulsive urges. None of this is incompatible with the notion that porn addiction rewires neural pathways and over-stimulates the appetite for novel partners. In some cases, however, the addiction is given extra traction by its ability to provoke OCD-like behaviour.

This may be what happened in the case of Fr O'Kelly and other addicts who amassed grotesque collections of pornography. Imagine taking the risk of hoarding those toxic images in your laptop and then not even having the time to look at them. What combination of genetic switches was thrown to produce that result? We don't know. But we can be certain that such intense sexual and moral chaos couldn't have been created without digital technology.

●

As I say, I've met the second priest who was caught with illegal porn. I'm not going to name him because, having read accounts of the court case, I think there's a chance that he downloaded child porn by accident. He was a gay man looking for pictures of young men having sex, and in the process of compulsive searching he saved three images (among hundreds) of underage boys. It was only right that he was suspended from ministry – but the magistrates didn't send him to jail, perhaps taking into account the massive naïvety of a man who used a shared parish computer to enter searches for 'twinks'. In court, the defence argued that he was very lonely and that, as a homosexual man who had taken a vow of celibacy, online porn was an irresistible short-cut to the only sexual pleasure available to him.

I know many Catholic priests and many of them are indeed desperately lonely. None of them strikes me as the sort of person who would commit offences against minors. But one or two of them do know their way around the world of internet pornography. A priest once told me: 'In honour of the feast of the Sacred Heart I'm removing my pornographic bookmarks from my computer.' It wasn't really a joke: he was using the landmark of the feast day as motivation to draw a line under a habit that he felt was becoming infuriatingly addictive as well as sinful.

A friend of mine, Shaun Middleton, is both a successful psychoanalyst and a Catholic priest. I asked him whether he thought the loneliness of the clergy made them susceptible to online pornography. 'Yes, definitely,' he said. 'When priests lived together in presbyteries there was less privacy. Now they're rattling around in these big houses with unoccupied rooms, and those empty spaces magnify their own feelings of emptiness. But the slide towards porn addiction can be very gradual. It can be triggered by something as trivial as a bad day.

'Let's say you've just married a couple, which arouses difficult feelings about your own loneliness and, frankly, you're feeling vengeful. Twenty years ago these men would have hit the bottle or started collecting antiques or gone on foreign holidays – anything to escape.

REDISCOVERING PORN

Now you've got the whole world at your fingertips through your laptop.'

You wouldn't have to change many details in this scenario, however, to apply it to other isolated men: a divorced schoolteacher might also start porn surfing where once he would have hit the bottle. Like other addictions, internet porn exploits loneliness. Also like other addictions, it can masquerade as an antidote to it. Drunks and drug addicts make friends with fellow users – but these friendships often consist of nothing more than sharing the experience of addiction with virtual strangers. It's a journey towards psychological and physical isolation: again and again, in AA meetings, you hear how alcoholics shrugged off the company of friends and then fellow drinkers and ended up with only the booze for company, alone in a living room or bedroom. Which is where, of course, porn addicts spend most of their time.

But internet porn isn't as straightforward as other objects of addiction. It seems to have a life of its own. The solo porn user is constantly 'meeting' new people, whether in the form of static images, characters in videos or participants in live streams; he can even talk to girls who will perform sex acts for him. Every major technological innovation, such as 3D movies, helps disguise the reality that he is being brought to orgasm by computer-generated images, not the touch of another human being.

From the moment porn went online, discussion boards and chat rooms appeared. Some of these operated like classified ads or down-market dating agencies. People used them to meet real partners, and although the results were often catastrophic – particularly for women who were rash enough to hang around the sites looking for boyfriends – these cases don't really come under the heading of addiction to internet porn. But much more common was the phenomenon of porn surfers with specific sexual obsessions converging on sites where they could talk to people with similar tastes and, by doing so, reinforce those obsessions.

Sociologists sometimes use the term 'plausibility structure' to describe networks of social support that make bizarre religious or political creeds seem reasonable. Generally speaking, the more deviant the belief, the more support it requires. People who worship green jellyfish need to surround themselves with a tight knot of fellow believers if they're to have a reasonable chance of keeping the faith.

Something similar happens with off-piste porn. Before the internet, people with unusual erotic desires would struggle to find material to sustain them. Now, however odd your fetish, you can find an image to turn you on – and other people who share your obsession.

Let's imagine that you are turned on by women in wheelchairs. A Google search quickly reveals 'Mad Spaz Club: Where There's a Wheel There's a Way', featuring 'paraplegic babes, quadriplegic and tetraplegic babes'. This site is a plausibility structure. It even comes with a postmodern mission statement: 'A disability can be beautiful as there is beauty in difference. Often impaired bodies are regarded as a subversive source of sensualism with intrinsic appeal because impairments provide a kaleidoscope of beauty beyond those embodied in cultural norms.'

REDISCOVERING PORN

The message is: your fix is part of who you are. Will Napier, a London-based psychologist who works at the Priory clinic, told me: 'We're seeing the growth of a particular culture in which your sexuality is a thing you discover. And key to this is the availability of ever more specialised pornography, ever more detailed and differentiated. Your preferences become part of a lifestyle that can be pieced together digitally. Once it becomes an issue of identity, then what's at stake is whether you're being true to yourself – and so authenticity becomes conflated with the satisfaction of every urge that happens to occur to you.'

●

To what extent do people *act out* fantasies that are nurtured by online pornography? Napier suggests that the combination of identity politics and digital stimulation puts pressure on people to seek out a lifestyle. 'If you discover online that people urinating on you is part of your sexuality, then the implication is that if you don't find a place where that can be done to you, you'll be fundamentally unfulfilled,' he says.

No doubt – but it's not only individuals with difficult-to-satisfy fetishes who feel unfulfilled when they try to move from porn to real-life sex. Heavy porn users in general report an inability to become aroused by real mates, and early onset of erectile dysfunction. Davy Rothbart of *New York* magazine interviewed dozens of male porn users and found a recurring theme. Stefan, a 43-year-old composer, said that when he had sex with his wife, 'I've got to resort to playing scenes in my head that I've seen while viewing porn. Something is lost there. I'm inside my own head.' Ron, a 27-year-old architecture student, said his porn habit was altering his relationship with his girlfriend. 'I guess I've been fading from her. It's like all the time with those porn stars was subduing my physical desire for my girlfriend. And, in some weird way, my emotional need for her, too.'[16] The problem here isn't so much that men are acting out porn fantasies. It's that they're trying to act them out but failing to find satisfaction.

This is the point at which internet porn addiction really begins to damage the lives of women. The number of women who look at porn compulsively is relatively small. That's probably because the female brain is less responsive to the prospect of multiple sexual partners. But women whose partners are habitual porn users find their sex lives disrupted in a number of different ways. Men who expect their digital women to press a particular combination of buttons can't get an erection unless real women press them, too. Which, understandably, real women are reluctant to do.

In addition, women come under pressure to meet physical expectations that have been moulded by porn. There have been plenty of stories in the media about adult women having breast implants and 'Brazilian waxes' so they look like porn stars. But far more troubling is the fact that young girls are trying to emulate the 'teen sluts' of cyberspace in order to ignite the porn-flavoured fantasies of teenage boys.

In fact, some women are finding it increasingly difficult to satisfy men, particularly those under 30. It's not their fault. Short of digitising themselves, there's no way they could fulfil the needs of their porn-obsessed partners. Why? Because, to put it bluntly, their boyfriends no longer want to have sex with human beings. Their brains have been conditioned by fantasy. Sex with another person can no longer produce the same rush of dopamine and endorphins that masturbating and orgasm in front of a computer can. This is the logical endpoint for both sexes of an addiction to internet pornography. In my opinion it's far more worrying than the much-discussed phenomenon of 'sex addiction', which strikes many commentators as just a trendy term for promiscuity.

Feminists in the 1980s used to talk about men being made redundant. They were there to inseminate women who wanted babies, but their roles as providers and guardians were negotiable, if not disposable. Now digital technology is tipping the scales violently in the other direction.

In Britain, more than a quarter of 14- to 17-year-olds go porn surfing every week. They're looking at videos of girls giving blow jobs and having anal sex. It may not be helpful to describe these boys as addicts, since there's nothing unusual about an uncontrollable adolescent sex drive. But they are being exposed to material that is designed to trigger addictive desires in older people, and this is undoubtedly making boys more sexually aggressive.

When teenagers talk to each other online, they reach for a pornographic vocabulary they've picked up from adult sites. This can cause the most pitiful confusion and embarrassment when they actually start dating. The boys associate sex with porn; they can't be bothered with, or don't understand, the usual courtship rituals. Simon Blake, chief executive of the Brook Advisory Centre, a sexual advisory service, reckons that young people struggle to come to terms with the expectations created by porn. 'Young people will come and say things like: Is it right, do I need to shave all my body hair off? Should I be making the other person scream? How do I make the other person scream?'[17]

•

Why are teenage boys watching hard-core porn in the first place? The simple answer is: because they can. Robert, the young publisher who arrived at a boys' boarding school in 2000, saw a revolution in the consumption of porn because the pupils got their hands on smarter technology. His successors have tablet computers and mobile phones that deliver an even smoother platform for watching rough sex. The boys didn't ask for iPads for Christmas because they wanted to see sluts being anally raped; they're watching these gross scenes because they were given iPads for Christmas. In other words, this is basically a supply-driven phenomenon, like so many addictions – the 18th-century gin craze, for example. But where the supply lines and symptoms of mass alcoholism are relatively easy to identify, 21st-century porn addiction is tangled up with the social and technological networks that nurture it. If the essential process of addiction is the replacement of people by things, then no other compulsion offers us so many different ways of making that self-destructive leap.

REDISCOVERING PORN

Since it was invented, porn has always turned people (usually women) into sexual images – that is, things. Now, thanks to computers, these images can depict real people performing real sex acts in real time. Admittedly, all the consumer is looking at is the surface of his monitor or mobile phone. But he's well aware of that – it's what he wants. Most people who bought 'dirty mags' saw them as a shabby substitute for face-to-face encounters; the medium itself wasn't an object of desire. In contrast, porn surfers often have a strangely intimate, possessive and protective relationship with technology.

For porn addicts, an upgrade can provide fresh sexual kicks: tablet computers are the perfect porn machines for the bedroom. The experience of viewing porn can be made to seem less dirty by the sheer smartness of the technology – the graceful contours of an iMac, the awesomely fast broadband, the cheeky ingenuity of the app. The thrill of owning these nice things may increase the dopamine reward provided by the porn. It's all part of the hit.

This addictive experience is evolving faster than our ability to monitor it, let alone limit the harm it causes. Looking at online porn is part of an activity now almost as inescapable as eating – using the internet. Xtube is never further away than a new tab on your browser.

To complicate matters, this endlessly malleable pornography is good at unlocking obsessive-compulsive urges. The collecting mania of some heavy porn users reflects an attempt to impose order on the world. Their sense of isolation goes beyond simply being starved of sex, just as the emptiness felt by people with eating disorders is more profound than physical hunger. Other individuals have a less tortured relationship with porn, but still find it sucking up incredible amounts of their time.

Never before have men had such easy access to the pleasure-giving chemicals associated with sex without having to go through rituals of courtship. Writing in the *Spectator* in January 2012, the philosopher Alain de Botton said he'd recently been at a dinner party in Gloucestershire at which 'three of my fellow males admitted they'd recently come through profound periods of internet porn addiction – not the mild curiosity one can expect, the sort where you can't wait to get home to look at the latest offering and are up till 3 a.m. every night'.[18]

We really don't know where this is leading. We can only guess. As the Conservative MP Claire Perry told the House of Commons in November 2010, 'a third of 10-year-olds have viewed pornography on the internet, while four out of every five children aged 14 to 16 admit to regularly accessing explicit photographs and footage on their home computers'.[19] No wonder that, as I said at the beginning of this chapter, internet porn is the addiction that comes closest to panicking the experts.

10

DELIVER US FROM TEMPTATION

Dr Adi Jaffe has blue eyes, immaculately combed fair hair and just the right length of designer stubble. He's wearing a beautifully cut, hand-finished jacket over faded jeans. He doesn't look much like a psychologist specialising in addiction, which is what he is. Sipping an espresso in one of Westwood's boutique cafés, he could be mistaken for a movie executive from nearby Hollywood. Or, if you have a vivid imagination, for a suave and well-connected drug dealer. Which is exactly what he used to be.

Jaffe turned a music recording studio into a front for the sale of high-grade crystal, powder and pills – until he got raided by a Beverly Hills SWAT team. After jail and rehab he went back to college and reinvented himself as an academic psychologist. Now, still in his early thirties, he's recognised as one of America's most persuasive thinkers on the subject of drug abuse. People listen to what he's got to say. After all, not many clinical researchers have been responsible for shifting, by his own estimate, hundreds of thousands of Ecstasy pills a year, to say nothing of the kilos of methamphetamine and, as he puts it, '*really good coke*'.

'I was very much a drug snob,' he explains.

Jaffe is intense, businesslike, sardonic. There's still a hint of a Tarantino character about him. You wouldn't have wanted to mess with him during his drug-dealing days. When he was busted, he refused to turn in his dealers. He preferred to do his time.

His drugs career started when he sold marijuana as a student in New York to pay for the lawyer he needed to defend him after a shop-lifting incident. I ask what he stole. 'Condoms,' he says, in a quiet voice. I look slightly confused. 'What?'

'You heard.'

He moved from New York to California and started dating a girl who was into rave culture and did Ecstasy every weekend.

I loved it. Really fun parties, great bunch of friends and my own recording studio. Back to dealing, but this time it was pills. It began with friends, but once you start selling drugs people quickly find out about you and come asking for some — and I've never been good at saying no.

So I went from a few dozen Ecstasy pills every other week to a hundred a month. Then a couple of hundred, and now I'm starting to make real money. Then I got introduced to speed, and when I started selling that stuff is when things really took off. [He started doing business with the cartels.]

DELIVER US FROM TEMPTATION

I needed a couple of guys to help me, and when the speed arrived we'd use it ourselves so we wouldn't have to sleep and miss out on sales. That recording studio became a veritable K-Mart for drugs. I was making $200,000 or $300,000 a year. I had a roster of 500 clients and I walked around with $10,000 in my pockets as spending money.

Plus, of course, I had an unlimited supply of any drug I wanted – I was smoking crystal meth constantly but somehow never ended up looking like those creatures in the meth ads. I was doing Ecstasy pretty much daily, eventually not even in pill form. When you buy and sell hundreds of thousands of pills, there's an incredible amount of pill dust at the bottom of the massive bags. So I'd smoke that with my cigarettes or meth. Like all good drug dealers, I had surveillance videos outside my studio, and when I look at the tapes I see that I've got a pipe in my hand nearly all the time.

Jaffe's days as Dr Feelgood came to an end when he got into a motor-cycle accident and the police found half a pound of cocaine in the lining of his jacket: when he came to in the hospital, he was chained to the bed. He detoxed in jail but started using immediately once he got out at the end of the week. When he kept refusing to co-operate by naming his dealers, an armed SWAT team kicked down his door and dragged him to jail to face 13 felony counts. After a year fighting the case, during which time he also got sober, Jaffe served only a year in jail. He detoxed in prison but started using again outside. It took a humiliating failed spell in rehab before he took a conscious decision to stop what he calls his lifelong self-sabotage.

Going back to college was his only realistic option. 'With nine felony counts on my record I wasn't even going to secure a job in a mall' he says. After much effort, he was accepted at UCLA, from where he gained his doctorate in the psychology of drug addiction.

Jaffe has a sophisticated understanding of brain chemistry that has led him into some sharp exchanges of fire with leading addiction experts. Unlike them, he knows exactly what it feels like to snort, swallow and smoke vast quantities of the substances they're talking about.

We talk for a bit about the legalisation of drugs. I have to be honest: this is a debate that really bores me, because it seems to belong to a different era, one in which governments assumed that whether a drug was legal or not made all the difference to people's readiness to consume it. Portugal, for example, makes a huge fuss about the success of its across-the-board decriminalisation of drugs, which it claims has greatly reduced the number of 'problem' addicts since 1998. And it's true that treating heroin addicts as patients rather than criminals has improved their health. But the flip side of this tolerance is that the number of people receiving treatment for addiction has grown by about a third, from 23,500 to 35,000. Even charity workers who work with heroin users worry that taking up the drug has become too easy.[1] Decriminalisation or legalisation changes the lines of supply and takes money out of the black market. But, in the final analysis, if a mood-altering drug is just as available as it used to be, then the number of people who become addicted to it is unlikely to fall.

These days most narcotics are easy to get your hands on if you're prepared to put in a minimum of effort tracking them down. As legal highs pour on to the market, the distinction between legal and illegal drugs is becoming ever more meaningless. The same is true of the legal classifications that distinguish hard from soft drugs. Politicians are confronted by new substances about whose long-term effects they know nothing. How are they supposed to classify pills that produce euphoria comparable to hard drugs but turn out to be no more toxic than soft Class C drugs? Or, for that matter, everyday prescription medications that turn out to have massive untapped potential for abuse? Every time an illegal lab in Bulgaria or Shanghai invents a sexy new party drug, the goalposts will have to be shifted again. (There's an interesting comparison to be drawn with the way the old categories of hard and soft porn have also become redundant, though in the case of pornography there's less room for confusion: as we've seen, hard-core material has become the norm.)

'The idea that we can "beat" the problem of drugs is just so misguided,' says Jaffe. 'For example, we've only just woken up to the fact that prescription drug abuse in this country is blowing up. People really want these medications. I always had customers for prescription pills – we had a guy working in a pharmacy who traded them for Ecstasy.

'Doctors are dealing in them. The Government is cracking down now, but Florida doctors were the laughing stock of America. They'd set up offices in mini-malls, and as you walked in there'd be a doctor on your right to write you a script and a counter on your left to dispense it.

'This is what the people who talk about legalisation of drugs don't acknowledge. The most commonly abused drugs are already the easiest to get hold of. You start with mom's Vicodin, or a kid shares his Ritalin with you at school – and the result is an epidemic level of abuse that we didn't even notice until about ten years ago.'

Jaffe's passion is for getting addicts into rehab – but not any old rehab: one that's based on a scientific understanding of the special challenges facing different sorts of addicts. In February 2011 he wrote a scathing article in the *Huffington Post* about the booming rehab business. 'Right now, it is too easy to sell the idea of recovery,' he wrote. The system was compromised by clinics that were incompetent, dogmatic or exploitative: 'You could easily check into a rehab facility and find they offer nothing more than an expensive 12-step programme. This is unacceptable. We have tools, like cognitive behavioural therapy and motivational enhancement therapy, which we know are effective. We just need to ensure they are part of the treatment model being offered to patients.'[2]

He has a simple model for illustrating the distribution of addictive behaviour in the population, which recognises that there is a continuous spectrum of such behaviour, but also draws attention to individuals whose overwhelming 'wanting' impulses mark them out from the rest of society. He uses the word 'disease' to describe their condition: I don't, but really it's a question of semantics, since he's aware of its diagnostic limitations and neither of us thinks addiction is by definition incurable – the 12-step dogma.

Jaffe draws a pyramid in which the bottom third is made up of ordinary people whose addictive impulses are difficult, but not impossible, to excite. Above them is a layer of vulnerable individuals whose natural reaction to stress is to search for a fix. At the apex are the addicts, with their wide-open 'wanting' pathways who are capable of developing an all-consuming obsession with anything from candy bars to sadomasochistic sex acts.

The pyramid is not a scientific model. As I hope this book has shown, we don't know enough about the reward mechanisms of the brain to predict who will end up at the top of the pyramid. If extreme addictive behaviours have a common biological cause, scientists have yet to discover it. For example, some addicts manifest symptoms of OCD while others don't; it's reasonable to infer from this that the neural pathways of the two groups have been disturbed in different ways, but that's about as far as we can go: any speculation about the relative importance of biology and environment is, as usual, guesswork.

I've talked a lot about dopamine in this book, because the discovery of its functions is bringing us closer to understanding apparently compulsive behaviour. But there is still no proof that a particular brain abnormality causes addiction.[3] If anything, the evidence points in the other direction: addictive behaviour, influenced above all by the available supply of addictive substances and experiences, can sometimes cause brain abnormalities. For example, brain-imaging technology is beginning to reveal how heavy cocaine use damages the axons or 'white matter' that transmit messages across the brain.[4] But observing this damage doesn't allow us to draw any conclusions about the extent to which the user was addicted to cocaine.

What we can say is that the acceleration of social development is pushing the internal boundaries of Jaffe's pyramid downwards. More of us find ourselves in the category of addict or the intermediary layer of vulnerable consumer. More of us are at risk than ever before of developing crippling addictive behaviours. Ignoring potentially harmful temptations involves significantly more willpower than it once did. Yet we're not necessarily aware of moving in the direction of addiction – and, when we do realise it, many of us are surprised.

Put it this way: it's as if someone or something has sneakily moved the boundaries of your self-control. For example, you didn't *ask* your local corner shop in Primrose Hill to start selling jumbo-sized Reese's Peanut Butter Cups. But there they are, right next to the cash register, as moreish as high-grade blow (or so I'm told). And you give in.

Nor can you remember precisely when your favourite pub started serving chilled white wine in huge glasses that mean that it takes only two journeys to the bar before you start feeling pissed, as opposed to three or four.

Nor did you invite big-boobed Belarusian bombshell Tanya into that pop-up at the bottom of your computer screen. I mean, how were you supposed to know that an exploratory click on Teenage Sluts Go Wild would hook you up to the camera in her bedroom?

Inside the pyramid, previously discrete technologies are getting mashed up to redraw the limits of acceptable behaviour. Exploiting our desire for the fix is fast becoming an interdisciplinary skill, as experts from the worlds of gaming, gambling, pornography, fast food and pharmaceuticals study each others' successes and pilfer what they can. Today's consumer electronics devices are the result of furious testing and wholesale theft from far less salubrious industries. Manufacturers are racing to create dopamine-tickling gadgets more compelling than their rivals'.

'Websites these days are all about targeting cues,' says Adi Jaffe. 'And I know that because I've been asked to help make them more addictive. Somebody I know personally is head of marketing for a set of gambling websites who wanted to use cues and triggers for bingo slot gambling games. He wanted to know how to persuade people who wouldn't normally play these games to try them out – and, once they were on the website, how to keep them spending money for longer.

'He knew I was an addiction expert and he wanted to buy my expertise to make his products more addictive. I said no. I'm not in the business of creating addicts any more.'

That's a smoking gun if ever I saw one. The online casino industry, in the days when it was still legal in the US, insisted that it wasn't trying to create addicts. But here we find the owners of an online casino trying to bribe a university psychologist to make their product more addictive. It would be interesting to know how many addiction specialists have been approached for the same purpose by the manufacturers of video games – and how many have agreed to share their expertise in return for a consultancy fee. Given that the world of addiction therapy is full of cowboys in the first place, I suspect the number is quite substantial.

●

In this book, I've concentrated on the spread of addictive behaviour in Britain and America. But globalisation is spreading variants of the same problem all over the world. We're moving closer to the moment when the fight against addiction and the crime that stimulates it will become a higher priority for the developing world than its ancient enemies, poverty and disease.

You can see the internal boundaries of Adi Jaffe's pyramid being pushed downwards in every modern society. People who were once immune to addiction find themselves at risk; those who were already at risk develop hard-core addictions. And those who were already at the top? They can get wasted on anything that takes their fancy, anywhere they like.

The past 25 years have witnessed the sudden disappearance of political and cultural obstacles that limited the geographical spread of particular addictive products and practices. The fall of the Berlin Wall, for example, was probably the single greatest gift to drug traffickers in the centuries-old history of their trade.

Misha Glenny describes in his terrifying book, *McMafia*, how the displacement of communist dictators by east European oligarchs and mafia has allowed drug dealers to flood emerging markets with amphetamines, Ecstasy, cocaine and heroin. There was never any shortage of chemists in the Eastern bloc; now their skills are being drawn upon and developed. At one point a Colombian cartel managed to smuggle one of its own top chemists into Bulgaria, with a specific brief to train Bulgarians in the production of cocaine. The unrefined drug itself was smuggled into Black Sea ports concealed in, among other things, shipments of mashed potato. The communist-trained chemical engineers could then turn it into powder for the fast-growing markets in Eastern Europe and Russia.[5] The demand for drugs is so great in Russia that amateur chemists are also flourishing, with horrible results. A synthetic opiate drug called krokodil, made from codeine-based headache pills, is so poisonous that it eventually turns the skin scaly, like a crocodile's. Flesh goes grey and peels off, so that heavy users can effectively rot to death. Incredibly, there's demand for it. And this in a country where 30,000 people already die from heroin addiction every year.[6]

New trade routes opened up by hi-tech organised crime have forced law enforcement authorities to tear up their old maps. For example, according to the US state department, the hub of global

Ecstasy trafficking is now Israel, where drug dealers have family links to gangs in all the major cities.[7]

Hi-tech globalisation has made it possible to shift drugs more safely and quickly. Computers allow dealers to manage their stock more efficiently, while the sophistication of international financial markets has increased the scope for money laundering. As we've seen, digital technology has hugely boosted the sale of legal highs, but it's also helped keep down the cost of cocaine and heroin, prices for which have roughly halved since 1990.[8]

One reason prices have dropped is the unprecedented migration of populations, which has moved dealers into new markets and sharpened competition. To pick just one example, the arrival of hundreds of thousands of Nigerians in the new South Africa has had disastrous consequences for local people vulnerable to substance abuse: Nigerian gangs have been working tirelessly to expand the consumption of drugs there.

Previously, each of South Africa's segregated communities had its own drug. Blacks smoked home-grown cannabis; coloureds smoked 'buttons', crushed mandrax tablets mixed with cannabis; and young whites used heroin or cocaine. Using a drug associated with another community was regarded as inappropriate, like breaking a taboo. But none of this made sense to the immigrant entrepreneurs. 'The Nigerian drug dealers identified early on that the market was ready for diversification, and so they started introducing different communities to new drugs,' writes Glenny.

'That meant making *dagga* [cannabis] more easily available to the coloureds and whites, while pushing the "buttons" beyond their traditional home of the coloured districts and townships. Black, white and coloured youth often came into contact with one another via the good offices of Nigerian suppliers.'[9]

The South African experience is replicated in many parts of the world, as migrant workers arrive suddenly in host communities – bringing economic benefits but also, in some cases, intoxicating substances which their new neighbours are only too eager to sample. Or it can work the other way round. There are thousands of migrant Chinese workers in Siberia, where they acquire a taste for cheap Russian vodka and carry it back home with them. Recently I spoke to a journalist from north-east China who said his home town was being devastated by 'Siberian drinking patterns'. He told me that the vodka used to be a rarity. 'Now this horrible cheap liquor – God knows what it's made from – is on sale in every store and is doing terrible damage. It has just cost me the life of my best friend.'

Organised crime isn't called 'organised' for nothing. Drug trafficking and people-smuggling are now carried out by the same criminal gangs: illegal migrants are forced to become drug mules.[10] In June 2010, Jan Brewer, Arizona's Republican governor, claimed that 'the majority of the illegal trespassers that are coming into the state of Arizona are under the direction and control of organised drug cartels'.[11] Her comment caused pious outrage, but it wasn't far from the truth.

In Latin America, Africa, Eastern Europe, the former Soviet Union, Afghanistan and parts of east Asia, central government has farmed out its responsibilities to the local mafia to an extraordinary degree. By an unhappy coincidence, many of these are also regions in which populations are moving from the countryside to the cities in greater numbers than ever before.

The dangers of such sudden demographic change are obvious. Unsurprisingly, the disorientation experienced by people uprooted from their home communities often encourages them to seek solace in chemical fixes. History is full of such unhappy episodes: the epidemic drunkenness of American Indians moved thousands of miles from their ancestral homelands is a famous example.

We still witness this phenomenon, to a greater or lesser degree, all over the world – including in Britain, where immigrant populations have brought their drug-taking and drug-dealing habits with them. In London, as in most large Western European cities, there's strong evidence that the open drug markets are dominated by ethnic minorities.[12] But, as in the new South Africa, substances are traded between communities, giving rise to a multicultural drug market that is also fed by a stream of postal deliveries from internet 'pharmacies'.

Despite the role played by organised crime, many young people regard unfamiliar drugs in the same way as they regard unfamiliar ethnic food. These things don't frighten them; not after a gap year spent in Thailand. Long-haul travel has changed the attitude of students and young professionals towards mind-altering drugs, which they have seen consumed in developing countries as part of the natural rhythm of life – or so they like to think, in their romantic way. Like strange and spicy dishes, the drugs belong to a menu of pleasures that grows longer every time they look at it – and from which, in their opinion, they have an absolute right to choose.

That sense of entitlement to pleasure dovetails nicely with the business plans of the providers of pleasure, both corporate and freelance. The movement of intoxicating substances around the world is more intricate and efficient than ever before. But it can never be fast enough for a generation for whom an unlimited choice of hedonic experiences is as natural as an unlimited choice of downloaded music – and for whom novel fixes are an indispensable part of life. This level of choice has only been available to young westerners for a few years; it remains to be seen whether it produces a cohort of middle-aged addicts – and, if so, what substances, objects or experiences will prove most addictive. Some of them may not have been invented yet. What can't be denied is that people born in the 1980s and 90s have access to a range of mood-fixing tools that is vastly greater than anything available to their parents, and that, in all likelihood, their children will have even more choices laid out in front of them.

●

This acceleration of availability isn't a generational change: it's happening faster than that. In the last five years alone, the burgeoning sophistication of consumer electronics has given birth to new obsessions and addictions that would have been unthinkable a decade ago. One way or another, everybody in the Western world has to confront the quickening of desire. It's true that many people can't afford to pursue more than a few of those desires. Most of us, however, face an intensity of temptation that we can only intermittently resist. Managing those temptations draws deeply on our psychological resources: it can dominate our thoughts and swallow up our time. Just look at the catatonic behaviour of shoppers in supermarkets faced with more choices than they can handle.

Some of us are quite happy zombies, though. After all, there are worse things than being spoilt for choice. The replacement of ancient social ties by customised objects and experiences isn't unwelcome. How many of us, hand on heart, really want to revert to the model of an extended family in which our recreational time is constantly interrupted by courtesy visits to distant relatives? We like small families and flexible friends with whom we enjoy mildly addictive pleasures, such as DVD box set marathons. Interestingly, middle-class viewers often talk about 'mainlining' episodes of series such as the cult Danish thriller *The Killing*.

You can spend a lot of time managing temptations before they represent any sort of problem. Indeed, we boast about our favourite fixes, because they convey information about us that we want other people to know. 'Mainlining' *The Killing* was a cool thing to do in the autumn of 2011 – especially so if you did it in bed, using your iPad, and remembered to drop it into conversation at work the next morning.

DELIVER US FROM TEMPTATION

This book has discussed the ways various pleasures overstretch the brain, becoming problems that we have to manage in a less enjoyable way. It's a spectrum: it isn't always easy to locate the moment mildly addictive behaviour becomes self-destructive, even in retrospect. What I find intriguing is that, when temptation becomes difficult to manage, people *continue* to identify themselves in terms of their tastes.

In some cases, even the most gruesome appetite disorders become badges of identity and honour. (Pippa from those AA lunchtime meetings was especially adept at turning her self-induced suffering into martyrdom.) Society makes this transition easier for us by teaching us that addictions are not so much the product of our actions as something we are unlucky enough to have acquired.

In the United States, going into alcohol or drug rehab has become a rite of passage for rebellious youths and, for adults, a form of sick leave to which barely any stigma is attached – especially as companies go out of their way to conceal what sort of treatment their employee is receiving. The roll-call of celebrities checking into rehab has even made these places seem glamorous.

In 2010, 2.6 million Americans received treatment at a rehab facility: 958,000 for alcohol abuse only, 881,000 for illicit drug use only, and 625,000 for both alcohol and illicit drug use. If the criteria are loosened to include any treatment for substance abuse, for example as an outpatient of a private doctor, then the total soars to 4.6 million people. No wonder that America's 'rehab industry' is worth an estimated $9 billion a year.[13] One telling detail: in 2012 the word 'rehab' was among the top

20 most expensive Google keywords – meaning that healthcare companies had bid huge sums in order to appear high up on the Google rankings when the word 'rehab' was entered into the search engine.[14]

Meanwhile, more and more British executives are being quietly packed off to recovery facilities. In 2011 an inquiry made under the Freedom of Information Act led to the revelation that the BBC had spent £19,000 at The Priory specifically to treat employees stressed out by cost-cutting initiatives; the actual total spent by the Corporation on rehab for its employees is thought to be vastly higher.[15] The Priory also sends psychiatrists to the City and to Canary Wharf to treat workers in the financial sector struggling with alcohol and cocaine addiction.[16]

Companies have been quietly paying for their top employees to dry out for decades, of course. What's different is a relaxed attitude to 'treatment' – an assumption that a period of recovery from addictive behaviour may form part of the natural arc of an employee's career. It's a price bosses are prepared to pay in exchange for their staff agreeing to work the punishingly long hours demanded by a globalised economy.

But they shouldn't expect things to run smoothly: nothing connected with addiction ever does. We've already seen that addicts in treatment centres have higher relapse rates than those not in treatment. We can argue about why this is – perhaps they were in a worse state to begin with; perhaps treatment is counterproductive – but the pattern of multiple sessions in rehab is a familiar one. Employers and insurance companies will normally only foot the bill for one rescue. Friends of mine who have been financially ruined by drug addiction blame the cost of treatment as much as the cost of the drugs.

Remember that, more often than not, recovery programmes incorporate the 12 steps. They're a potent formula, but not always in a productive way: they can persuade people going through a temporary crisis that they're saddled for life with a non-existent disease. For some individuals, that's a recipe for learned helplessness. For the less scrupulous providers of 'specialist' care, it's a recipe for lucrative repeat business, as addicts fork out the remains of their savings – or their parents' savings – for just one more spell in rehab.

The problem of helplessness isn't confined to addicts. Governments display ostentatious anxiety about the mental and physical wellbeing of their citizens, and use it to justify endless exercises in social engineering. These don't necessarily work, but they manage to spread public anxiety about the dangers of losing control of our appetites. And the funny thing is that we don't really mind being nagged in this way. We hate being taxed by the government – but this focus on our wellbeing doesn't cause offence because it acknowledges that we have a tough time resisting temptation. To an extent, it absolves us from our sins.

The effort to keep our minds and bodies in good shape is now so central to our existence that a new type of identity politics is emerging that may supersede the old markers of class and ethnicity, particularly as society becomes more multicultural.

Recently I attended a few meetings of something called the 'pan-fellowship', a 12-step group in west London that doesn't limit its meetings to any one addiction. I was surprised by how smoothly it worked. Speakers seemed to draw strength from each other's battles against appetites and emotions, without worrying too much about the precise nature of the 'addictions' that had led them there. The amount of cross-addiction was impressive. ('My name's Sarah and I'm an alcoholic and cocaine addict with food issues.') Just as striking was the diversity of the gathering: the attendees were a far more mixed bunch than you'd find in the average workplace or congregation. It made me reflect that addiction really is an equal-opportunities employer, with a potential for shaking up society that we're only now beginning to appreciate.

You can see the change happening on daytime TV chat shows as well as around the dinner tables of Manhattan and Kensington. Instead of defining themselves in terms of social and ethnic background, people often reduce themselves to a bundle of addiction management strategies. Learned helplessness isn't fun, exactly, but it certainly gives us something to talk about.

●

Modern addiction has the overtones of a social movement: the numbers of people involved are so vast and the direction of travel so clear. One of the many reasons political ideologies seem irrelevant is that people are too busy coping with their own bodily dilemmas to invest in grand narratives. The self-absorption one encounters in 'the rooms' of various programmes is not strikingly different from the cognitive style of millions of men and women outside them. And I don't think it's a coincidence that today's most successful religious movements are those that exploit people's anxieties about their appetites or tap into addict-centred identity politics – possibly both at the same time.

Addiction has the ability to mould religious beliefs even in the rainforests of South America. In 1999 I had a vivid encounter with a Peruvian peasant cult which was expecting something astonishing to happen in the year 2000. Led by an illiterate shoemaker called Ezequiel, who had anointed himself their Messiah, these 'Israelites of the New Universal Covenant' were waiting for the last Inca emperor, Atahualpa, to waken from his sleep in the Amazon jungle. Then Solomon's Temple would rematerialise in the intoxicatingly thin mountain air of Machu Picchu, the Inca city in the skies. The *Israelitas* dressed like the Old Testament Jews they had seen depicted in ancient Hollywood epics. On assignment for a magazine, the American photographer Victor Balaban and I hired a boat to travel 100 miles down the Amazon to the Israelites' colony, Alta Monte. We were greeted by tiny, leather-faced old men dressed like Charlton Heston in *The Ten Commandments*. They took us by torchlight through the jungle to the cult's newly thatched temple; inside, the crowd of worshippers parted for us, bowing deeply.

I was there to ask the Israelites about their extraordinary apocalyptic prophecies. But that wasn't what they wanted to discuss. Instead, their stories were about recovery from drugs and alcohol. They were nearly all Andean peasants who had drifted into Lima when the economy fell apart, and most of them had become addicts. Interestingly, the only English speaker in the colony had picked up the language while working as a drug dealer in Miami. 'I had a white stretch limo until I started the freebasing,' he said. But the Israelites had cleaned him up and now he was sober with a wife and two daughters.

The Israelites have recently undergone changes: since my visit, Ezequiel has died (failing to fulfil his promise of rising from the dead). But they are still a presence in Peru and, despite their eccentricities, still employing the same recipe of all nearly successful Latin American religious movements – one of deliverance from alcohol and drugs.

Much the same is true in fast-growing churches all over the world. I don't think I've ever visited an African or West Indian Pentecostal church that didn't devote a lot of time and effort to keeping their members and their families free from drugs and alcohol – and this is true whether the congregation is based in Nigeria, Jamaica or Britain.

In America, meanwhile, the most successful churches pay meticulous attention to worshippers' appetites – and their anxieties about them. We're encouraged by the media to think of fundamentalist and evangelical churches as backward-looking. But the reality is that their vision of personal salvation borrows heavily from the secular world's relentless emphasis on the self. In the stores attached to the churches, believers can buy DVDs, video games, satellite subscriptions and other fixes that mediate their supposedly direct 'personal relationship with

Jesus'. Issues with alcohol, drugs or prescription medication? Try Christian rehab. Ashamed of your bulging waistline? Join a Christian slimming club. (Presumably members are steered away from the popular 'Jesus cupcakes' on which the Lord is depicted in icing sugar.)

The 12 steps started life as Christian 'moral rearmament' and are easily converted back into evangelical Christianity by interpreting the Big Book's 'higher power' as Jesus. The 12-step-based Christian Track Program, founded in America in 1991, is endorsed by 3,500 churches. Christian treatment centres use it, and it's also available as an option in secular rehab facilities, in much the same way as kosher food is available on plane flights.

Be warned, though: Bible-based recovery isn't any cheaper than the regular variety. The Capstone treatment centre in Arizona offers a Christian residential programme for troubled young men aged 14 to 24 who struggle with 'chemical dependency, substance abuse, sexual addiction, trauma, family conflict, and personal problems including loss, hurt, anger, abuse, depression, low self-esteem, defiance and a rebellious attitude'. The cost? An upfront payment of $17,500, plus two further instalments of $14,850 each. Capstone's theology is straight-down-the-line evangelical Protestant, and its therapeutic philosophy is similarly dogmatic: parents are informed that addiction is an irreversible brain condition, 'something similar to diabetes'.[17] That is a thoroughly misleading claim, I'd argue – but if you're spending that sort of money perhaps it's reassuring to learn that you're up against a truly powerful enemy.

In London, the thriving middle-class charismatic congregations are full of young men and women who used to take drugs and who, without skilful pastoral supervision, could easily be tempted to started again. A few years ago, I attended a service at one of London's most successful Anglican charismatic churches. Essentially it consisted of a sequence of spiritual hits in the form of rock songs and slick stand-up routines – perfect for producing dopamine spikes in the audience of born-again Christian hipsters. One particularly intense testimony came from a man called Charlie whom, I suddenly realised, I had last seen puking his guts out of a window of the Randolph Hotel, Oxford, one May Morning in the early 1980s.

Here's a prediction: any established religion that fails to help people with appetite management issues will be pushed out of the market-place in the next few decades. By the same token, any religion that can place the recovery of physical health, good looks and appetite control at the centre of its spirituality stands a very good chance of attracting followers. Movements may still choose to define themselves in terms of their doctrines. But, in practice, their growth will depend on their ability to mould their teachings around our narcissistic anxieties. The interesting question is whether they will do so by challenging or exploiting those anxieties. Sometimes it can be hard to tell the difference.

●

DELIVER US FROM TEMPTATION

Throughout history, rapid social change has encouraged commentators to adopt an apocalyptic frame of mind – unsurprisingly, since nearly all doomsday prophecies, religious and secular, involve an uncontrollable acceleration of events before the End. I've written extensively about these beliefs, so I don't want to fall into the trap myself when confronting the very different subject of addiction.

In many respects, the quickening of change has been a blessing. The second half of the twentieth century witnessed a sharp fall in deaths from starvation and the infectious diseases that have plagued humanity for millennia. Our growing obesity is less dangerous than it would once have been, thanks to improvements in medical care. In less than a decade, heart attacks in Britain have halved, in part owing to protective statins developed by the 'evil' Big Pharma, anti-smoking legislation and better informed hospital treatment.[18]

But, while welcoming these improvements, we need to ask ourselves whether they aren't creating space for more insidious attacks on our freedom. For example, have we given serious thought to the question of artificial enhancement of our living experiences? There are already 'happiness classes' in some of Britain's most competitive schools, many of whose pupils will also be having their happiness chemically enhanced thanks to a diagnosis of ADHD. Think back to the Adderall pills that Ivy League students are swallowing like Smarties in order to gain a tiny but crucial edge over their academic competitors. Suppose that an authoritarian country, obsessed with its position in the educational and economic league tables, decides to force attention deficit drugs down the throats of its schoolchildren. As we've seen, these medications are as likely to inflict long-term brain damage as they are to enhance the intellect – but they may provide a quick cognitive fix that boosts productivity. Will liberal democracies take a self-sacrificing decision not to embrace this Brave New World? (In Aldous Huxley's 'negative utopia', as he described it, everyone takes a state-produced drug called soma that produces intervals of perfect spiritual pleasure. The rest of the time they're mostly shopping or having recreational sex; being alone is a source of shame.)

One thing is for sure: certain newly developed countries will have no such scruples. Nor will multinational corporations looking to outsource production to the most efficient partners they can find – meaning those whose employees can stay awake longest as their bosses turn them into speed addicts.

The awkward truth is that the acceleration of technological progress can't be divorced from the faster production of addictive substances and experiences. This dilemma was brilliantly set out by Paul Graham, a Silicon Valley investor and blogger, in an online article published in 2010. His short essay, 'The Acceleration of Addictiveness', makes the point that if we want to stop the processes that addict us, we will also have to call a halt to the experiments that cure diseases. That is because they are products of the same research.

'Technological progress,' he states, 'means making things do more of what we want. When the thing we want is something we *want* to want, we consider technological progress good. If some new technique makes solar cells more efficient, that seems strictly better. When progress concentrates something we don't want to want – when it transforms opium into heroin – it seems bad. But it's the same process at work.'[19]

The world is more addictive than it was 40 years ago, explains Graham: food, drink, drugs, television and computers are more engaging than ever before. As a result, we've got into the habit of liking things too much. 'As far as I know, there's no word for something we like too much,' he says. 'The closest is the colloquial sense of "addictive".' In future, he predicts, anyone who wants to avoid addiction will be condemned to 'a kind of lonely squirming'. We will increasingly be defined by our willingness to refuse temptation.

Graham is on to something important here – but his theory works better if we replace the notion of liking things too much with that of wanting them too much. It's not the experience of pleasure that is accelerating in the modern world: it's the experience of desire, prompted by environmental cues that continue to tantalise us even when the pleasant feelings arising from consumption have evaporated.

As shorthand for our habit of wanting things too much, the colloquial sense of 'addictive' is perfectly adequate. Indeed, the imprecise, colloquial way we refer to addiction corresponds more closely to modern reality than supposedly scientific definitions of addiction that reduce it to biologically determined behaviour produced by a (non-existent) disease.

Everybody is theoretically at risk of developing addictive habits, because the stimulation of desire is associated with primitive and vulnerable areas of our brains. Most of us are familiar with the feeling that our appetites are controlling us rather than the other way round. It's something we struggle against. And that struggle is shaping our lives as profoundly as the struggle against poverty and disease shaped those of our ancestors.

The modern consumer economy is partly fashioned around our inability to exercise willpower. That economy preys on us but also rewards us, since we are part of it and depend for our livelihoods on other people's vulnerability to temptation. That is not so much a value judgment as a statement of fact. The multiplication of choice, the expansion of the free market and the stimulation of greed are so tightly interwoven as to be almost indistinguishable from each other.

We can't realistically extricate ourselves from the exploitation of desire: it's fundamental to all social development. On the other hand, we should be aware that we've created an environment for ourselves that seeks to tease out our latent addictive instincts. That teasing process has become so relentless that we scarcely notice it. Whether we're buying a chocolate bar or a house, the gravitational pull towards *things* that expand our appetites is getting stronger. You could even argue that all the recent innovations in global financial services have been designed to produce a degree of dependence on credit that would be familiar to any street-corner drug dealer.

DELIVER US FROM TEMPTATION

We sometimes hear the claim that, as a society, we've become 'addicted' to spending and to consumer goods. That's too vague a generalisation to be useful. A better way of putting it would be to say that the 'addictive personality' – the familiar term for people who take refuge in short-term sensory rewards – is fast becoming the default personal style of disorientated modern citizens. This isn't to say that we can easily measure and categorise people's personalities: the results of such exercises are rarely convincing. We are a long way from being able to identify future addicts, and it's not clear that we will ever be able to do so. But what I hope this book has illustrated is the *direction* in which we're moving – towards government by desires that, thanks to a fundamental mismatch between the evolution of our bodies and the evolution of society, have a tendency to run out of control.

Fortunately, powerful desire doesn't lobotomise us. In the final analysis, addiction is a disorder of choice, and we're not doomed to carry on making bad choices to the point of helplessness. The challenge is identifying those bad choices. For me, back in the spring of 1994, that wasn't so difficult: I'd become sufficiently addicted to alcohol that becoming teetotal felt like being released from prison. But most people drawn into compulsive patterns of behaviour aren't in such a desperate situation and can't identify a single substance or experience whose renunciation will change their lives. Instead, they struggle to untangle an assortment of addictive urges from the healthy or harmless stimulation of their appetites. That is not an easy thing to do.

THE FIX

Perhaps we need to rediscover the vigilance that protected our hunter-gatherer ancestors. The quicker we are to spot the technological tricks that manipulate our 'wanting' impulse, the greater will be our chance of resisting them.

That's if we want to, of course.

NOTES

1. CUPCAKES, IPHONES AND VICODIN

1 Jerry Cacciotti and Patrick Clinton, 12th Annual Pharm Exec 50, PharmExec.com, 1 May 2011.

2 Craig Nakken, *The Addictive Personality: Understanding the Addictive Process and Compulsive Behaviour*, Hazelden, 1996, pp. 11–13.

3 Judson A. Brewer and Marc N. Potenza, 'The Neurobiology and Genetics of Impulse Control Disorders: Relationships to Drug Addictions', *Biochemical Pharmacology* 75: 1, 2008, pp. 63–75.

4 Emma Forrest, 'Cupcake Wars', *Daily Telegraph*, 14 April 2005.

5 http://www.whyeat.net/forum/threads/15092-I-baked-my-b-f-I-am-sorry-cupcakes

6 Abigail Natenshon, 'Bulimia Nervosa: Symptoms, causes, recovery', http://www.empoweredparents.com/1eatingdisorders/bulimia.htm

7 http://www.facebook.com/sprinkles

8 Lisa Baertlein and Mary Slosson, 'The Crumbs cupcake trade: boom or bubble', Reuters, 30 June 2011, http://www.reuters.com/article/2011/06/30/us-ipo-crumbs-idUSTRE75T4WF20110630

9 See Carlo Colantuoni, Pedro Rada, Joseph McCarthy, Caroline Patten, Nicole M. Avena, Andrew Chadeayne, Bartley G. Hoebel, 'Evidence that Intermittent, Excessive Sugar Intake Causes Endogenous Opioid Dependence', *Obesity Research* 10, 2002.

10 Dan Hope, 'iPhone Addictive, Survey Reveals', *Live Science*, 8 March 2010, http://www.livescience.com/6175-iphone-addictive-survey-reveals.html

11 Jesse Young, 'Apple's attention to detail', *Flood Magazine*, 14 October 2010, http://floodmagazine.com/2010/10/14/apples-attention-to-detail/

12 Dan Bloom, 'iPhone Addiction Disorder hits Taiwan', TechEye.net, 17 November 2010, http://www.techeye.net/science/iphone-addiction-disorder-hits-taiwan

13 Sarah Lacy, 'Angry Birds Tops 200 Million Downloads', Techcrunch.com, 18 May 2011, http://techcrunch.com/2011/05/18/angry-birds-tops-200-million-downloads-more-than-double-its-crazy-forecast-tctv/

14 Peter Vesterbacka, interview with Milo Yiannopoulos at Virtual Goods Summit, London, 11 November 2010.

15 John House, M.D., 'House vs. House: Vicodin Addiction and Hearing Loss', ABC News, 20 September 2008, http://abcnews.go.com/Health/PainNews/story?id=5841784

16 Ann Oldenburg, 'Friends star Matthew Perry's Addiction to Vicodin is latest Hollywood vice', *USA Today*, 8 March 2001, http://www.opiates.com/media/vicodin-addiction-usatoday.html

17 Frazier Moore, Associated Press, 'Viewers feel Dr House's pain', 12 May 2005, http://today.msnbc.msn.com/id/7832799/ns/today-entertainment/t/viewers-feel-dr-houses-pain/

18 Terra Naomi, *The Vicodin Song*, http://www.youtube.com/watch?v=rlWH9uICH-Q

2. IS ADDICTION REALLY A 'DISEASE'?

1 Ernest Kuntz, *Not-God: A History of Alcoholics Anonymous*, Hazelden, 1979, p. 22.

2 Brendan I. Koerner, 'Secret of AA: After 75 Years, We Don't Know How It Works', *Wired*, July 2010, http://www.wired.com/magazine/2010/06/ff_alcoholics_anonymous/all/1

3 ASAM, Public Policy Statement: 'Short Definition of Addiction', 12 April 2011, http://www.asam.org/

4 Jacob Avery, 'Complicating Addiction: What is the role of Micro-Sociology?', paper presented to the American Sociological Association, 2008.

5 Stanton Peele, 'The Top Ten Problems with the "New" Medical Approach to Addiction', http://www.peele.net/blog/110711.html

6 Stanton Peele, 'Hail the Revelation', *The Guardian*, 18 October 2006, http://www.guardian.co.uk/commentisfree/2006/oct/18/drugsandalcohol.society

7 Jennifer Mattesa with Jed Bickman, 'A New View of Addiction Stirs up a Scientific Storm', *The Fix*, 16 August 2011, http://www. thefix.com/content/addiction-gets-medical-makeover8004

8 John Booth Davies, *The Myth of Addiction*, second edition, Routledge, 1997, pp. 47–8.

9 Peggy J. Ott et al, *Sourcebook on Substance Abuse: Etiology, epidemiology, assessment, and treatment*, Allyn & Bacon, 1999, p. 255.

10 Daniel Akst, Interview with Gene M. Heyman: 'Is Addiction a Choice?', *Boston Globe*, 9 August 2009, http://www.boston.com/ bostonglobe/ideas/articles/2009/08/09/qa_with_gene_m_ heyman/

11 The surveys were the Epidemiological Catchment Area Study 1980–84, the National Comorbidity Survey 1990–92, the National Comorbidity Survey 2001–03 and the National Institute on Alcohol Abuse and Alcoholism study of substance abuse 2001–2.

12 Gene M. Heyman, *Addiction: A Disorder of Choice*, Harvard University Press, 2009, pp. 69–74.

13 Alfred W. McCoy, *The Politics of Heroin: CIA Complicity in the Global Drug Trade*, 1991, http://www.scribd.com/doc/50124993/ Alfred-W-McCoy-The-Politics-of-Heroin-CIA-Complicity-in- the-Global-Drug-Trade-1991#page=158

14 Peter Brush, 'Higher and Higher: American Drug Use in Vietnam', *Vietnam* magazine, 15, No. 4, December 2002.

15 Lee Robins, 'Vietnam veterans' rapid recovery from heroin addiction: A fluke or normal expectation?', *Addiction*, 88, 1993, pp. 1041–1954.

16 Michael Gossop, *Living with Drugs*, Sixth Edition, Ashgate, 2007, p. 33.

17 Ibid., p. 33.

18 Peter Brush, op. cit.

3. WHAT THE BRAIN TELLS US (AND WHAT IT DOESN'T)

1 Patrick McNamara, 'Is there a Parkinsonian Personality?', About. com, http://parkinsons.about.com/od/faqs/f/parisons_personality.htm

2 Kent C. Berridge, '"Liking" and "wanting" food rewards: Brain substrates and roles in eating disorders', *Physiology & Behaviour* 97, 2009, pp. 537–50.

3 University of Michigan news service, 'Why wanting and liking something simultaneously is overwhelming', 1 March 2007, http://ns.umich.edu/new/releases/3165

4 Anna Rose Childress, 'What Can Human Brain Imaging Tell Us about Vulnerability to Addiction and to Relapse?', *Rethinking Substance Abuse*, ed. William R. Miller and Kathleen M. Carroll, Guilford Press, 2006, pp. 46–7.

5 'Parkinson's treatment linked to gambling addiction', *Sunday Times* (Perth), 2 April 2011, http://www.perthnow.com.au/news/western-australia/parkinsons-treatment-linked-

to-gambling-addiction/story-e6frg13u-
12266032505575

6 'Parkinson's Patients Shed Light On Role On Reward Bias in Compulsive Behaviors', *Science Daily*, 16 Jan 2010, http://www.sciencedaily.com/releases/2010/01/100113122251.htm

7 Norman Doidge, *The Brain that Changes Itself: Stories of Personal Triumph from the Frontiers of Brain Science*, Penguin, 2007, p. 107.

8 Harvey B. Milkman and Stanley G. Sunderwirth, *Craving for Ecstasy and Natural Highs: A Positive Approach to Mood Alteration*, SAGE, 2010, p. 38.

9 L. Stinus et al, 'Nucleus accumbens and amygdala are possible substrates for the averse stimulus effects of opiate withdrawal', *Neuroscience*, 37, Issue 3, 1990, pp. 767–73.

10 William Burroughs, *Naked Lunch*, Penguin, 1972, xiii.

11 Morten L. Kringelbach, *The Pleasure Center*, Oxford University Press, 2009, p. 57.

12 Dirk Hansen, 'The Nucleus Accumbens, Addiction Inbox', http://addiction-dirkh.blogspot.com/2010/02/nucleus-accumbens.html

13 Harvey B. Milkman and Stanley G. Sunderwirth, op. cit., p. 122.

14 Norman Doidge, op. cit., p. 114.

15 Joseph Frascella et al, 'Shared brain vulnerabilities open the way for nonsubstance addictions: Carving addiction at a new joint', *Annals of the New York Academy of Sciences*, Vol. 1187, February 2010.

16 Gene M. Heymann, op. cit., p. 143.

NOTES

17 David Eagleman, *Incognito: The Secret Lives of the Brain*,
    Canongate, 2011, p. 107.

18 S. Barak Caine et al, 'Role of Dopamine D2-like Receptors in
    Cocaine Self-Administration: Studies with D2 Receptor Mutant
    Mice and Novel D2 Receptor Antagonists', *Journal of
    Neuroscience* 22 (7), 2002, pp. 2977–88.

4. ENTER THE FIX

1 Christine Bradley, 'Why do you want an ugly duckling?',
    http://realtyjoin.com/christineinatl/2011/03/29/
    why-do-you-want-an-ugly-duckling/

2 Morten L. Kringelbach, *The Pleasure Center*, Oxford University
    Press, 2009, p. 5.

3 Gad Saad, *The Consuming Instinct: What Juicy Burgers, Ferraris,
    Pornography, and Gift Giving Reveal about Human Nature*,
    Prometheus Books, 2011.

4 Kenneth Burke, *Language as Symbolic Action*, University of
    California Press, 1966, p. 16.

5 World Health Organisation, fact sheet on diabetes, August 2011,
    http://www.who.int/mediacentre/factsheets/fs312/en/

6 Jessica Warner, *Craze: Gin and Debauchery in an Age of Reason*,
    Random House, 2003, p. 22.

7 Elise Skinner, 'The Gin Craze: Drink, Crime & Women in 18th
    Century London', *Cultural Shifts*, 17 November 2007, http://
    culturalshifts.com/archives/168

8 Nicholas Christakis and James Fowler, *Connected: The Amazing Power of Social Networks and How They Shape Our Lives*, Harper Press, 2011, p. 22.

9 Malcolm Gladwell, *The Tipping Point: How Little Things Can Make a Big Difference*, Little, Brown, 2000, p. 160.

10 Gene M. Heyman, *Addiction: A Disorder of Choice*, Harvard University Press, 2009, p. 26.

11 Jacob Avery, 'Complicating Addiction: What is the role of Micro-Sociology?' – paper presented to the conference of the American Sociological Association, 2008.

12 'Casino Rituals', *Ace-Ten Blackjack Resources*, http://www.ace-ten.com/casinos/rituals

13 'Yes, Bayer Promoted Heroin for Children', *Business Insider*, 17 November 2011, http://www.businessinsider.com/yes-bayer-promoted-heroin-for-children-here-are-the-ads-that-prove-it-2011-11?op=1

14 Stuart Walton, *Out of It: A Cultural History of Intoxication*, Penguin Books, 2002, p. 113.

15 Gary S. Becker, Kevin M. Murphy and Michael Grossman, 'The Market for Illegal Goods: The Case of Drugs', *Journal of Political Economy*, Vol. 114, February 2006, pp. 38–60.

16 Gabor Maté, *In the Realm of Hungry Ghosts: Close Encounters with Addiction*, North Atlantic Books, 2010, p. 111.

5. WHY CAKE IS THE NEW COKE

1 Statistics on obesity, physical activity and diet, NHS Health and Social Care Information, 2011.

2 Jane Black, 'Fast Food's Dirty Little Secret: It's the Middle Class Buying Burgers', *The Atlantic*, 2 December 2011, http://www.theatlantic.com/life/archive/2011/12/fast-food's-dirty-little-secret-it's-the-middle-class-buying-burgers/249308/

3 Robert H. Lustig, Laura A. Schmidt and Claire D. Brindis,' Public health: The toxic truth about sugar', *Nature* 482, pp. 27–9, February 2012.

4 Michael Gossop, *Living with Drugs*, Sixth Edition, Ashgate, 2007, pp. 199–200.

5 Nicole M. Avena, Pedro Rada, and Bartley G. Hoebel, 'Evidence for sugar addiction: Behavioral and neurochemical effects of intermittent, excessive sugar intake', *Neuroscience and Biobehavioral Reviews 32*, 2008, pp. 20–39.

6 'Krispy Kreme 3Q Net Up 97% On Higher Revenue, Same-Store Sales', *Wall Street Journal*, http://online.wsj.com/article/BT-CO-20111130-716535.html

7 India Knight, 'Here's our chance to run poor shopping out of town', *Sunday Times*, 18 December 2011.

8 http://www.marksandspencer.com/Our-Food-Policies-About-Our-Food-MS-Foodhall-Food-Wine/b/56421031

9 David A. Kessler, *The End of Overeating: Taking control of our insatiable appetite*, Penguin, 2009, pp. 26–7.

10 Ibid., p. 147.

11 Ibid., p. 127.

12 Martin R. Yeomans, 'Learning and Hedonic Contributions to Human Obesity', in *Obesity: Causes, Mechanisms, Prevention, and Treatment*, ed. Elliott M. Blass, Sinauer Associates, 2008.

13 T.J. Gilbert et al, 'Obesity among Navajo adolescents: relationship to dietary intake and blood pressure', *American Journal of Diseases of Children* 146 (1992), pp. 289–95.

14 Peter C. Whybrow, *American Mania: When More Is Not Enough*, W.W. Norton, 2006, pp. 141–7.

15 Ibid., p. 144.

16 Calum MacLeod, 'Obesity of China's kids stuns officials', *USA Today*, 1 September 2007, http://www.usatoday.com/news/world/2007-01-08-chinese-obesity_x.htm

17 Andrew Jack, 'Brazil's unwanted growth', *Financial Times* magazine, 8 April 2011, http://www.ft.com/cms/s/2/6e0319c2-5fee-11e0-a718-00144feab49a.html#axzz1hBC54Aaf

18 David A. Kessler, op. cit., p. 177.

6. HAPPY HOUR

1 Murray Wardrop, 'Police release CCTV footage of drunk woman rolling under train in Barnsley station', *Daily Telegraph*, 22 December 2011.

2 Sarah Nathan, 'The Take That effect: How middle-aged fans go mad when the ageing boy band comes to town', 17 June 2011, *Daily Mail*, http://www.dailymail.co.uk/femail/article-2004447/The-Take-That-effect-How-middle-aged-fans-react-ageing-boy-band-comes-town.html

3 John Carvel and Mary O'Hara, 'Binge drinking Britain: surge in women consuming harmful amounts of alcohol', *Guardian*, 6 May 2009.

4 Tracy Clark-Flory, 'The rise of binge drinking women', *Salon*, 9 December 2010, http://www.salon.com/2010/12/09/binge_drinking_2/

5 National Women's Law Center, National Report Card 2010, http://hrc.nwlc.org/states/national-report-card

6 National Health Service, Statistics on Alcohol, England 2010, http://www.ic.nhs.uk/pubs/alcohol10

7 Tracy Clark-Flory, op. cit.

8 Danielle M. Dick et al, 'Rutgers Alcohol Problem Index Scores at Age 18 Predict Alcohol Dependence Diagnoses 7 Years Later', *Alcoholism: Clinical and Experimental Research*, Vol. 35, Issue 5, May 2011.

9 Jamie Bartlett and Matt Grist, *Under the influence: What we know about binge-drinking*, Demos, 2011, p. 19.

10 Institute of Alcohol Studies, *Trends in the Affordability of Alcohol in Europe*, http://www.ias.org.uk/resources/papers/occasional/uk-affordability-trends.pdf

11 Michael Gossop, *Living With Drugs*, Sixth Edition, Ashgate, 2007, p. 77.

12 Alicia Wong and Sufian Suderman, 'Binge drinking "emerging issue in Singapore" says HPB', *Today*, 17 December 2008, http://www.channelnewsasia.com/stories/singaporelocalnews/view/396865/1/.html

13 http://www.moviegoods.com/spring_break/

14 *Wasting the Best and the Brightest: Substance Abuse at America's Colleges and Universities*, National Center on Addiction and Substance Abuse at Columbia University, 2007, http://www.casacolumbia.org/templates/Publications_Reports.aspx#r11

15 Harvey B. Milkman and Stanley G. Sunderwirth, *Craving for Ecstasy and Natural Highs: A Positive Approach to Mood Alteration*, SAGE, p. 170.

7. DRUGSTORE COWBOYS

1 Mikaela Conley, 'Adderall drug shortage will continue in 2012, government officials say', ABC News, 3 January 2012, http://abcnews.go.com/blogs/health/2012/01/03/adderall-drug-shortage-will-continue-in-2012-government-officials-say/

2 'Demi Moore Took Adderall Too Before Her Seizure!', PerezHilton.com, 26 January 2012, http://perezhilton.com/2012-01-26-demi-moore-adderall-seizure#.TyfH3WBmzIY

NOTES

3 'L. Alan Sroufe, Ritalin Gone Wrong', *New York Times*, 28 January 2012, http://www.nytimes.com/2012/01/29/opinion/sunday/childrens-add-drugs-dont-work-long-term.html?pagewanted=all

4 J.D. Colliver et al., 'Misuse of Prescription Drugs: Data from the 2002, 2003, and 2004 National Surveys on Drug Use and Health, Office of Applied Statistics, 2006'.

5 http://www.justanswer.com/criminal-law/1p6c6-recently-arrested-adderall-pills-without-prescription.html

6 Russell Newcombe, 'Zopiclone: Assessment of the consumption and consequences of zopiclone (Zimovane) among drug-takers in a north-east town', Lifeline Publications, 2009.

7 Paul Gerrard and Robert Malcolm, 'Mechanisms of modafinil: A review of current research', *Neuropsychiatric Disease and Treatment*, August 2007 Volume 2007:3 (3), pp. 349–64.

8 Jonah Lehrer, 'Trials and Errors', *Wired*, UK edition, February 2012.

9 *Scotsman*, 'MoD's secret pep pill to keep forces awake', 27 February 2005, http://www.scotsman.com/news/health/mod_s_secret_pep_pill_to_keep_forces_awake_1_1387967

10 http://www.thedailybeast.com/articles/2012/01/25/faking-adhd-gets-you-into-harvard.html

11 Margaret Talbot, 'Brain Gain', *The New Yorker*, 27 April 2009, http://www.newyorker.com/reporting/2009/04/27/090427fa_fact_talbot

12 Ibid.

8. GAMING, THE NEW GAMBLING

1 'Internet Addiction?', Tokyo Housewife Blog, http://tokyohousewife-ashley.blogspot.com/2011/12/internet-addiction.html

2 Julia Keefer, 'Cyber Housewives Addicted to the Internet: How it Negatively Affects Spousal Relationships in Web-Friendly American Households Today', http://www.nyu.edu/classes/keefer/twenty/lee2.html

3 'Taiwan man dies playing video games at internet cafe: police', AFP, 6 February 2012, http://www.smh.com.au/digital-life/games/taiwan-man-dies-playing-video-games-at-internet-cafe-police-20120206-1r0ck.html

4 I. Nelson Rose, 'The Unlawful Internet Gambling Enforcement Act of 2006 Analyzed', *Gaming Law Review*, December 2006, 10(6): 537–41, http://www.liebertonline.com/doi/abs/10.1089/glr.2006.10.537

5 Interview with Milo Yiannopoulos, January 2012.

6 Ryan van Cleave, *Unplugged: My Journey into the Dark World of Video Game Addiction*, HCI, 2010.

7 Tamara Lush, 'At war with World of Warcraft: an addict tells his story', *Guardian*, 29 August 2011, http://www.guardian.co.uk/technology/2011/aug/29/world-of-warcraft-video-game-addict

8 'Call of Duty sets five-day sales record', AFP, 19 November 2011, http://www.dawn.com/2011/11/19/call-of-duty-sets-five-day-sales-record.html

NOTES

9 'The World of Warcraft rehab clinic', 7 January 2009, *SK Gaming*,
http://www.sk-gaming.com/content/21188-The_World_of_
Warcraft_rehab_clinic

10 Marcus Yam, 'Rehab Center Help Kicks WoW Habit for $14,000',
Tom's Hardware, 8 September 2009, http://www.tomshardware.
com/news/wow-world-warcraft-addition-rehab,8613.html

11 'Rehab available in U.S. for Web addicts', AP, 7 September 2009,
http://www.statesman.com/business/content/business/stories/
technology/2009/09/07/0907internetaddiction.html

12 Brenna Hillier, 'Psychological study evaluates Angry Birds
addiction', VG247, 13 September 2011, http://www.vg247.com/
2011/09/13psychological-study-evaluates-angry-birds-addiction/

13 WOW DETOX, http://www.wowdetox.com/view.
php?number=55590

14 WOW DETOX, http://www.wowdetox.com/view.
php?number=55599

15 Amy Muise, Emily Christofides, and Serge Desmarais, 'More
Information than You Ever Wanted: Does Facebook Bring Out
the Green-Eyed Monster of Jealousy?', *CyberPsychology &
Behavior*, August 2009, Vol. 12, No. 4: 441–4

16 Tom Bissell, 'Video games: the addiction', *Observer*, 21 March
2010, http://www.guardian.co.uk/theobserver/2010/mar/21/
tom-bissell-video-game-cocaine-addictiom

17 http://online.wsj.com/article/SB10001424052970203806504577181351486558984.html

18 http://www.dailymail.co.uk/femail/article-2080398/Facebook-cited-THIRD-divorces.html

9. REDISCOVERING PORN

1 Benjamin Wallace, 'The Geek-Kings of Smut', *New York* magazine, 7 February 2011.

2 Samuel Pepys's diary, 8 February 1668, *The Shorter Pepys*, Penguin Books, 1993, p. 873.

3 Andy Beckett, *Guardian*, 26 November 2009, http://www.guardian.co.uk/technology/2009/nov/26/dark-side-internet-freenet

4 Sharna Olfman, *The Sexualization of Childhood*, Greenwood, 2009, p. 126.

5 Gail Dines, *Pornland: How Porn has Hijacked our Sexuality*, Beacon, 2010, p. xvii.

6 Benjamin Wallace, op. cit.

7 Blake Robinson, 'Pornography and Socially Responsible Investing', *Public Discourse*, 27 October 2010, http://www.thepublicdiscourse.com/2010/10/1910

8 Gail Dines, op. cit., p. 49.

9 Judith Reisman, '2004 Testimony: The Science Behind Pornography Addiction', http://www.drjudithreisman.com/archives/2011/06/2004_testimony.html

10 Daniel Linz, statement submitted to US Senate Committee on Commerce, Science, and Transportation, 2004.

11 Ryan Singel, 'Internet Porn – Worse Than Crack?', *Wired*, http://www.wired.com/science/discoveries/news/2004/11/65772

12 Norman Doidge, *The Brain that Changes Itself: Stories of Personal Triumph from the Frontiers of Brain Science*, Penguin, 2007, p. 108.

13 Interview with the author, October 2011.

14 Bill Clegg, *Portrait of an Addict as a Young Man*, Jonathan Cape, 2010.

15 Shame of the priest addicted to porn, 14 March 2002, http://www.getreading.co.uk/news/s/3043_shame_of_the_priest_addicted_to_porn

16 Davy Rothbart, 'He's Just Not That Into Anyone', *New York* magazine, 7 February 2011.

17 Eleanor Mills, 'OMG: Porn in Cyberspace', *Sunday Times*, 19 December 2010.

18 Alain de Botton, Diary, *Spectator*, 28 January 2012.

19 *Hansard*, 23 November 2010, http://www.publications.parliament.uk/pa/cm201011/cmhansrd/cm101123/debtext/101123-0003.htm

10. DELIVER US FROM TEMPTATION

1 Peter Beaumont, 'What Britain could learn from Portugal's drugs policy', *Observer*, 5 September 2011, http://www.guardian.co.uk/world/2010/sep/05/portugal-drugs-debate

2 Adi Jaffe, 'Drug Rehab Treatment: America's Broken System', *Huffington Post*, 11 February 2011, http://www.huffingtonpost.com/adi-jaffe-phd/drug-rehab-treatment-_b_819683.html

3 Stanton Peele, 'Nora Volkow Explains (Not Really) Why People Don't Become Addicted', *Psychology Today*, 7 February 2012, http://www.psychologytoday.com/blog/addiction-in-society/201202/nora-volkow-explains-not-really-why-people-dont-become-addicted

4 Adi Jaffe, 'The brain after cocaine – white matter damage and addiction treatment', 23 June 2010, http://www.allaboutaddiction.com/addiction/brain-cocaine-white-matter-damage-addiction-treatment

5 Misha Glenny, *McMafia: Seriously Organised Crime*, Vintage, 2009, pp. 56–8.

6 Shaun Walker, Krokodil, 'The drug that eats junkies', *Independent*, 22 June 2011, http://www.independent.co.uk/news/world/europe/krokodil-the-drug-that-eats-junkies-2300787.html

7 Glenny, op. cit., p. 140.

8 Claudia Costa Storti and Paul De Grauwe, 'Globalization and the Price Decline of Illicit Drugs', CESifo Working Paper No. 1990, May 2007, www.SSRN.com

9 Glenny, op. cit., pp. 216–17

10 Jeffrey Kaye, *Moving Millions: How Coyote Capitalism Fuels Global Immigration*, Wiley, 2010.

11 Ginger Rough, Brewer, 'Most illegal immigrants smuggling

drugs', *Arizona Republic*, 25 June 25, 2010 http://www.azcentral. com/news/articles/2010/06/25/20100625arizona-governor-says-most-illegal-immigrants-smuggle-drugs.html#ixzz1l2e6tImb

12 Kevin Marsh, Laura Wilson, Rachel Kenehan, 'The impact of globalization on the UK market for illicit drugs', CESifo, 2008.

13 Results from the 2010 National Survey on Drug Use and Health: Summary of National Findings, U.S. Department of Health and Human Services, http://oas.samhsa.gov/ NSDUH/2k10NSDUH/2k10Results.htm#7.3

14 'Revealed: Google's Top 20 Most Expensive Keywords', PPC Blog, http://ppcblog.com/most-expensive-keywords/

15 Katherine Rushton, 'BBC spends £19,000 treating stressed out staff at The Priory', *Daily Telegraph*, 11 February 2012 http://www. telegraph.co.uk/culture/tvandradio/bbc/9074284/BBC-spends-19000-treating-stressed-out-staff-at-The-Priory.html

16 Simon Goodley, 'Markets meltdown leads to surge in City addictions', *Guardian*, 9 September 2011, http://www.guardian. co.uk/business/2011/sep/09/addiction-drugs-alcohol-city-london

17 http://www.capstone treatmentcenter.com/getting_started/ problem.html

18 http://www.dailymail.co.uk/health/article-2091879/Heart-attack-deaths-halve-years-fewer-smokers-better-care.html

19 Paul Graham, 'The Acceleration of Addictiveness', July 2010, http://www.paulgraham.com/addiction.html